OPEN YOUR BIG, BOLD BEAUTIFUL MOUTH!

How to Use Your Words to Unleash God's Power

M. Alphonso Belin and A.J. Polizzi

WestBow
P R E S S
A DIVISION OF THOMAS NELSON

All Scripture quotations, unless otherwise noted, are taken from the HOLY BIBLE, NEW INTERNATIONAL Version® (NIV). Copyright © 1973, 1978, 1984 by International Bible Society. Used with permission of Zondervan. All rights reserved.

Scriptures noted AMP are taken from the Amplified® Bible. Copyright © 1954, 1962, 1965, 1987 by The Lockman Foundation. Used with permission.

Scriptures noted MSG are taken from THE MESSAGE: The Bible in Contemporary Language®. Copyright © 1993, 1994, 1995, 1996, 2000, 2001, 2002. Used with permission of NavPress Publishing Group.

Scriptures noted NASB are taken from New American Standard Bible®. Copyright © 1960, 1962, 1963, 1968, 1971, 1973, 1975, 1977, 1995 by The Lockman Foundation. Used with permission.

Scriptures noted KJV are taken from The King James Version of the Bible. Copyright © 1979, 1980, 1982 by Thomas Nelson Publishers. Used with permission.

WestBow Press books may be ordered through booksellers or by contacting:

WestBow Press
A Division of Thomas Nelson
1663 Liberty Drive
Bloomington, IN 47403
www.westbowpress.com
1-(866) 928-1240

Because of the dynamic nature of the Internet, any web addresses or links contained in this book may have changed since publication and may no longer be valid. The views expressed in this work are solely those of the author and do not necessarily reflect the views of the publisher, and the publisher hereby disclaims any responsibility for them.

Any people depicted in stock imagery provided by Thinkstock are models, and such images are being used for illustrative purposes only.

Certain stock imagery © Thinkstock.

ISBN: 978-1-4497-3775-7 (sc)
ISBN: 978-1-4497-3774-0 (hc)
ISBN: 978-1-4497-3776-4 (e)

Library of Congress Control Number: 2012900971

Printed in the United States of America

WestBow Press rev. date: 06/04/2012

CONTENTS

Part I
The Heart of Faith: Inner Foundations

Part II
The Voice of Faith: Outward Expression

Part III
The Command of Faith: Commanding Expression

Part IV
The Gratitude of Faith: Thankful Expression

PREFACE

For more than thirty years, Alphonso Belin has traveled the world bringing God's principles of faith and message of Christ to men and women across the globe. From the United States to South Africa, from England to Sweden, from Turkey to the South Pacific, he has carried God's Word so people everywhere could learn how to overcome obstacles and enjoy a life filled with God's blessings.

I met Alphonso when he was starting out in the ministry. I still remember our first meeting: Here was an energetic young man from small-town Florence, South Carolina, who was going to change people's lives. He had no doubts about it; he was going to change and advance the lives of men and women by teaching them God's principles and precepts of faith. It was God's call for his life.

I didn't know it then, but Alphonso and I would become life-long friends. For almost thirty years, it's been my honor to enjoy his friendship and benefit from his counsel, generosity, and calling.

When Alphonso and I talked about the vision for this book, I immediately knew this was a project I had to get involved with. We both envisioned a book that offered men and women a full set of principles and tools for change based on God's Word. A book that didn't just raise important questions but provided a proven game plan for action.

The result is what you now hold in your hands. From start to finish, this book tackles real-life problems by teaching people step-by-step how to release God's power and blessings into their life by speaking faith-filled words. It's a book which offers readers both the wisdom and the tangible practices for creating the meaningful and victorious life God has promised each of us.

God's message in this book has changed my life deeply; I know his message will do the same for you.

A. J. Polizzi

Introduction
"Bless You Boys!": A City Speaks

"Words kill, words give life; they're either poison or fruit—you choose."

—*Prov. 18:21*

"Handle them carefully, for words have more power than atom bombs!"

—*Pearl Strachen Hurd*

April 10, 1984—the city of Detroit was abuzz. Spring was in the air; the long, dreaded winter had officially passed. It was time for a new season and new dreams.

More importantly, it was time once again for baseball, Tigers baseball. Yes, it was opening day at Tiger Stadium!

The crowds arrived early and jammed the ballpark as they always did for the home opener. Young and old, white collar and blue collar, students, doctors, lawyers—everyone had skipped out on work or school early to watch the Tigers play. They wanted to be outside; they wanted to see their team. They wanted to step into the moment and be part of the sights and sounds of Tigers baseball.

No one was thinking about the economy, the sky-high interest rates, the fifteen-percent unemployment, or the relentless problems that had settled over Detroit's auto industry for more years than anyone cared to remember. That day, it didn't matter. That day, the Motor City was about baseball—and only baseball.

Besides, this opening day was different: The Tigers were coming home undefeated, with a 5-0 winning record. Not since 1911 had the Tigers gotten off to such a bold start. It was a record-book beginning, and it seemed that team manager Sparky Anderson's preseason prediction "that something tremendous is gonna happen" might be more than optimistic banter. Perhaps the Tigers would overcome the mediocrity of past seasons and become winners again. That was the hope, anyway.

As the Tigers took the field on that special day in April 1984, the sold-out stadium rumbled with excitement. On the mound was Tigers' pitcher Dan Petry. The crowd watched closely as Petry pawed the soft soil with his cleats, his eyes transfixed on the opposing batter, who was crouched and ready at the plate. Suddenly, the entire stadium grew silent. Petry wound up and hurled the opening pitch.

In a brilliant flash, the ball zoomed across the plate. The batter tried to react—he wanted to react—but it was too late. The ball thudded into the well-worn contours of the catcher's leather glove. "Strike!" bellowed the plate umpire to confirm the indisputable result.

Zoom, thud, strike! It was a pattern that would repeat itself over and over that day before the hometown crowd. Pitch after pitch, the opposing players fell. Inning after inning, they toppled over like cascading dominoes.

And with each falling domino, the Detroit fans celebrated. They cheered. They clapped. They roared. When Tigers' slugger Darrell Evans launched a three-run home run blast to secure a commanding lead, the fans began dancing in the aisles and standing on their seats. From the first inning to the last, it was a day of celebration.

But the celebration didn't stop there—the Tigers kept winning. By the end of April, the team was 18-2; by May, an astounding 35-5. Tom Monaghan, the pizza baron who had purchased the team only months before the start of the 1984 season, was nearly speechless as every sportswriter and news agency pressed him for comments about the team.

While Monaghan searched for the right words, the Detroit fans had no trouble finding them. They knew exactly what to say: "Bless you boys!" poured out of their mouths. Every fan, every person, every household took hold of those magnificent words. "Bless you boys! Bless you boys!": The words filled the city. People wouldn't stop saying it; people couldn't stop saying it.

As the momentum grew, newscasters and pundits tried to pinpoint who or what had started the "Bless you boys!" ball rolling. Many claimed a local sportscaster had planted the seed a few years earlier when he used the phrase to ironically preface his criticisms about the Tigers and their poor performance. Others speculated it may have been an avid fan in the bleacher seats who helped advance the matter by routinely calling out his "Bless you boys!" encouragement while holding up a John 3:16 sign.

In the end, however, it didn't really matter how the trend got started. What mattered—all that mattered—was the realization of everyone in Detroit that it was a time of blessings. Innately, people knew it, and they didn't want it to end. "Bless you boys!" was what they grabbed on to for their team, their city, and themselves. The words had an impact. The words made sense. The words needed to be said.

I know because I was there. Only a few years out of Bible school, I was in metro Detroit that year teaching and preaching in many of the local churches and community bible groups. I, too, got caught up in the "Bless you boys!" phenomena. I wanted to say it. I needed to say it. Yes, it had to be said.

What irony. Before 1984, I'd only heard negative stories about Detroit. Having been raised in the small town of Florence, South Carolina, I knew little about big cities, let alone Detroit. I had no idea what to expect, and I was leery about what I'd encounter.

The reality I experienced in Detroit was entirely different from the stories I'd heard. I experienced firsthand a city filled with incredibly warm, generous, and caring people. They embraced me. They helped me. They made me feel welcome and at home. And they were fervently proud of their families, homes, and communities.

To top it off, there I was—young Alphonso Belin from small-town America—immersed in a metropolitan community of millions, where everyone spoke words of encouragement and blessings. I had never experienced anything like it, not on that scale.

Not even in my Bible groups and church assemblies had I witnessed such fervency and passion over the importance of speaking beneficial words. An occasional "Bless you" or "God bless you"—yes, that was spoken in the churches, but nothing like what happened in Detroit that year. The entire city of Detroit was tuned in and involved, somehow awakened to the impact and importance of the words being spoken.

What took place in Detroit during that special baseball season of 1984 left an indelible mark on me. It jolted my awareness and encouraged me on a journey to learn as much as I could about God's wisdom as it relates to our words.

Before that season, I thought I knew all there was to know about words. After that season, I realized there was much more I needed to learn.

With an almost disturbing sense of urgency, I began to revisit and reexamine the many biblical principles surrounding the impact and importance of our words. I had to grab hold of God's wisdom on this subject and put it fully into practice in my own life. From there, I could teach others how to put those principles into practice in their own lives.

Words—Your Life's Instrument

So why are our words so important? What wisdom will we explore together in this book?

In the Bible, God specifically tells us, "Words kill, words give life; they're either poison or fruit—you choose" (Prov. 18:21 MSG). That's God's blunt, frank, and indispensable wisdom for each of us.

Life or death, encouragement or discouragement, bright light or dark clouds, words—our words—determine the outcome. Help or hurt, blessing or curse, building up or tearing down, through words—our words—we decide the result. The words we speak sit at the center of all we do. They propel our journey and steer our course. They shape our life and the lives of those around us.

In a dramatic and echoing perspective on the impact of our words, poet Pearl Strachen Hurd said, "Handle them carefully, for words have more power than atom bombs!"

Hurd's comparison and cautionary advice are biblically spot on. Our words, like atom bombs, have a devastating impact and critical consequences on every level—spiritually, intellectually, emotionally, and physically. No quality or dimension of life remains untouched by them. For good or for bad, their shock waves stretch far and wide, beyond what even our eyes can see.

Concerning their importance, God told us that he used words to create our universe and everything in it. "By faith we understand that the universe was formed at God's command, so that what is seen was not made out of what was visible" (Heb. 11:3).

To create it all, God opened his mouth and said something—and what he said came to be. His invisible words created the visible, the tangible, the monumental.

Like God, we were designed to be a people of words. In his own image and likeness, God fashioned us this way—as speakers, authors, and articulators on the earth. Words are his gift to us, our instrument for creating, building, and shaping all that is around us.

As we study and begin to understand the significance of our words and their consequences, the question for each of us to answer becomes this: What are we doing with the gift of our words?

Are we using our words to advance our life or limit it? Support our goals or undermine them? Help or hurt others?

If we're not succeeding and achieving our goals, we need to examine what we're saying. If we're losing ground or struggling in certain areas, we need to look at the words we routinely broadcast. If we're floundering rather than flourishing in our homes, jobs, and personal relationships, we, most likely, need to change our words to change the result.

WORDS—GIVING VOICE TO YOUR FAITH

These same questions must be asked and answered in our spiritual life as well. What words are we speaking? Are we expressing words of faith in God and Jesus Christ or words of doubt? Are we declaring the divine blessings they specifically promised to each of us or are we saying something else?

In this book, we will learn that the Christian life of faith was designed by God to be a life of vibrant, outward expression. From our heart and willing mouth, God has asked us to express our trust in him and our belief in all his promises. These words of faith will change our circumstances and bring us countless blessings. These words will lift us out of problems and get us past every concern.

Of all the words we will ever speak, the words of faith are the most powerful, dynamic, and life changing.

Through numerous Scripture passages, multiple examples, and various vantage points, we will learn about these faith-filled words. We will learn that what we believe on the inside—in our heart—must be expressed on the outside in order to secure the results we desire.

We will explore the vital connection between our heart and our mouth and learn how they work together, one internalizing God's promises and the other externalizing them—and together grabbing hold of God's blessings for our life.

In every detail, God has a plan and a purpose for us to succeed. We have his word on it. In fact, through the great work that is the Bible, he's given us hundreds and hundreds of his promises to trust and believe. But to experience the fullness of these promises, we must say something. We must give a voice to our faith. Through our words as well as our deeds, we must put our faith into action.

WORDS—YOUR HEAVENLY PRONOUNCEMENTS

In this book, we will learn about another distinguishing feature of our words and faith. We will learn that every Christian has been given the right to speak on behalf of God and Jesus Christ and pronounce heaven's blessings on the earth.

The specific term for this right is "authority." We've been given authority by God and Christ to speak as their agents, with the full force and unlimited resources of their kingdom supporting our words.

For Christians, heavenly authority unlocks a world of new insights and opportunities. It represents our right to declare victorious outcomes for our life, family, and community. It represents our right to command obstacles and problems to move aside. It signifies our ability to speak the words "God bless you!" and to have God respond to our pronouncement with his incomparable blessings.

How did we obtain this special right to speak, this authority of heaven? As we will learn, it came when we accepted Jesus Christ and became members of God's royal family. It's one of the many gifts we received, all part of our new life and heritage in Christ.

I hope you're excited to learn. When you begin to understand your authority to speak on behalf of God and Christ and to issue specific commands and pronouncements backed by their power and might, your speech will never be the same. This understanding will impact what you say and how you say it.

WORDS—EXPRESSING YOUR GRATITUDE

In this book, we will explore one other important group of faith-filled words. We will examine the words of gratitude—our words of thanks and praise to God. We will learn how valuable these words are to him and how vital these words are for our life.

Our words of thanks and praise accomplish so much. They generously give back to God. They support our faith life. They even usher in more of heaven's blessings for our lives.

In many rich and rewarding ways, these words open up a vast channel of expression, one that allows us to voice every promise and provision of our Christian heritage.

Once you learn about these words, I'm certain you will add them to your spiritual vocabulary. I know these words of gratitude will transform your life forever. Never again will you look at your life or your circumstances as you did before.

OUR FOUR-PART JOURNEY TOGETHER

This is a life-changing book—at least that's my intended goal. I want to challenge and inspire you to use your words wisely, effectively, and profoundly so they move your life forward in a positive direction with all the help, support, and blessings God has for you.

This is also a how-to book. Through specific steps, exercises, and examples, I'll show you how to use your words. Step by step, chapter by chapter, I'll provide you with the tools and underlying principles you need to immediately begin using your words effectively. Not tomorrow but today.

To accomplish these goals, this book has been organized into four parts. Each part lays the necessary foundation for the lessons, principles, and exercises that come later. This way you will have in your hands a comprehensive guide to follow, one that contains every resource you need to build, grow, and change.

THE 1984 DETROIT TIGERS—A SEASON OF DREAMS?

Are you curious about how that season ended? Was it a season of dreams or just a whole lot of hype?

The 1984 "Bless You Boys" Tigers went on to become one of the greatest teams in baseball history. They won the divisional title with a record of 104 wins, fifteen games ahead of the second-place contender. They became the American League Champions by sweeping the Kansas City Royals in the playoffs.

The team's victory march continued in the World Series, where the Tigers won the crown by trouncing the San Diego Padres four games to one. It was a record-book season that stunned Major League Baseball and captured both the awe and imagination of the entire nation.

The team achieved one other notable, almost unfathomable record that year: The Tigers became the first baseball team in more than fifty-seven years—not since the legendary 1927 New York Yankees with Babe Ruth and Lou Gehrig—to be in first place from the first day of the season to the last. An astonishing, wire-to-wire, first-place leader and finisher!

In his book *Wire to Wire,* longtime Detroit sportswriter and acclaimed news columnist George Cantor described the '84 Tigers' season as "the avalanche of 1984—as overpowering as it was inexplicable." It was, he wrote, as if "a daisy cutter full of dreams had been dropped on Detroit."

I know many years have passed since that special season in Detroit, but I'm certain it's time for "a daisy cutter full of dreams" to be harvested once again—and not just in Detroit but in every city, every home, and every life. It's time for each of us to speak and receive the incredible dreams and blessings God has for us. It's surely time.

Let's learn how.

PART I

THE HEART OF FAITH

INNER FOUNDATIONS

1

Your Relationship of Trust

"Trust opens the door to change."

—Peter F. Drucker

"Faith is a living, daring confidence in God's grace, so sure and certain that a man could stake his life on it a thousand times."

—Martin Luther

Foundations are the most important part of any structure, building, or enterprise. Whatever we seek to create or accomplish is determined by the quality and strength of our foundation. If our foundation is defective or deficient, whatever we erect simply won't last. It will, in the end, waver, crumble, and fall.

The foundation for our journey together in this book is faith. Everything we build together in these pages rests on it. Faith is what binds this manuscript from cover to cover.

Thankfully, we have God's promise that faith is the best foundation—the strongest, the most secure, the unshakable. "It is by faith you stand firm," God tells us (2 Cor. 1:24).

It's our guide for every aspect of life, from the words we speak to the tasks we undertake. "We live by faith, not by sight" (2 Cor. 5:7).

So what then is this thing we call faith? How do we define it? How do we capture its meaning so we can apply it to our everyday living?

Quite simply, faith is trusting God. Though we don't see God with our eyes, we trust that he exists. Though we can't reach out to touch him with our hands, we trust that he is continually watching over us. Though we live temporarily on the earth and he lives in heaven, we trust that his goodness, wisdom, and power are available to us and for us.

In the book of Psalms, King David beautifully describes this trust with a simple example. Focusing on the mistaken trust people often place in human strength and physical resources, David explains:

> Some trust in chariots and some in horses, but we trust in the name of the Lord our God. They are brought to their knees and fall, but we rise up and stand firm. (Ps. 20:7-8)

Updating David's example with today's technology and modern resources, we could rephrase his statement on faith by saying, "In the problems and battles of life, some people put their trust in laptop computers, software programs, and corporate solutions, but we— God's people of faith—put our trust in the Lord, our God. They experience continued disappointment and devastating crashes, but we rise up from all our challenges to live solid, successful lives."

The book of Hebrews adds further wisdom to the central message of faith by explaining that trusting God is the firm foundation for everything beneficial in life. So paramount is this placement of our trust that one contemporary translation of Hebrews calls it "the fundamental fact of existence" for creating and enjoying a life worth living (Heb. 11:1 MSG).

Trust in God is our home base, our firm foundation for everything in life. By trusting him, we stand on solid footing with a secure handle on all that is good, useful, and valuable for our lives. By trusting him, we are guided and supported in all matters, even those we can't see or grasp with our physical senses.

When we understand this elemental concept of trust, the other details, principles, and precepts of faith—the lessons and discussions we will explore together throughout this book—fall into place and proper context. These principles, precepts, and teachings simply become extensions of our trust in God. Nothing more, nothing less.

The message of faith isn't complicated. We don't need a Harvard degree to understand its meaning or grow wise in its wisdom. Faith, at its core, is about trusting God.

GROWING AND BALANCED TRUST

Life was never intended to be static. Everything in life has been designed to grow and mature, our faith included.

In the Bible, God encourages us to grow in faith by telling us to trust in him with all our heart. We are to trust and lean on him fully rather than place our confidence in mankind's limited knowledge and imperfect thinking:

> Trust in the Lord with all your heart and lean not on your own understanding; in all your ways acknowledge him, and he will make your paths straight. (Prov. 3:5-6)

God guides us further on the path of growth and maturity by telling us in the book of Hebrews to come forward and draw near with complete trust and total confidence:

5

Let us all come forward and draw near with true
(honest and sincere) hearts in unqualified assurance
and absolute conviction engendered by faith, [that is,
by that leaning of the entire human personality on
God in absolute trust and confidence in His power,
wisdom, and goodness]. (Heb. 10:22 AMP)

Look at the key words used here: "unqualified assurance," "absolute
conviction," the "leaning of the entire human personality on God."
These are decisive and uncompromising terms that set a high
benchmark for a strong and mature faith. The words fully capture
the unshakable bond our trust can grow into as we walk with God.

Also think about these words as they relate to your life and the
people who have been part of it. Has there ever been someone in
your life whom you've trusted with an "absolute conviction" or an
"unqualified assurance"? If you've been fortunate to have even one
person like this in your life, even for a short period of time, you
know what a treasured relationship you could lean on and enjoy.

With a special person like this in your life, would you be willing to
lean back, even to the point of falling? Would you trust the person
to catch you? Yes, of course. An exercise like this would be easy
because of your inward assurance, your unshakable trust.

This same assurance is what God wants us to develop in him. He
wants us to lean fully on him, confident that he will catch us each
and every time and in every circumstance. He wants us to know
with absolute conviction that he will never let us fall.

What else does God's word in Heb. 10:22 teach us about our maturing
and growing faith?

Importantly, this Scripture highlights the three main pillars of our
trust: trust in God's power, trust in God's goodness, and trust in

God's wisdom. Each of these pillars or supports is necessary for our stability and security.

For example, how secure would you be if you trusted only in God's power but not in his goodness or wisdom? Would you be able to lean on him with absolute and unqualified assurance in every situation facing you or your family?

Or consider another example where you trusted only in God's goodness but not in his wisdom or power. How secure would your trust be? Could you lean on him with complete confidence? Would you be certain that help and rescue were close at hand? No, of course not.

In these examples, you would find yourself surrounded by doubt and constant worry. Like a circus clown, you'd be wobbling and flailing about on a stool with legs of grossly different lengths, anxiously awaiting your impending fall with the absolute conviction and unqualified assurance of the crash about to occur.

God's grace is a seamless package that incorporates all that he is: infinitely good, wise, and powerful. Our trust must balance on these three mighty pillars. Only by trusting in the fullness of God's limitless being will our faith and our life be balanced, stable, and secure in every situation and every circumstance.

God summarized this perfectly for us when he said, "Stop trusting in man, who has but a breath in his nostrils. Of what account is he? I have made you and I will carry you. I will sustain you and I will rescue you. I am God, and there is no other; I am God, and there is none like me" (Isa. 2:22; 46:4, 9).

TRANSFORMING TRUST

As we move along faith's path and experience God's powerful, wise, and loving hand in our life, our trust in him will grow and strengthen.

And with this growth, our trust will eventually transform into something even more enduring: a deeply personal relationship.

This is faith's ultimate goal—our ultimate goal. It's here, within this personal relationship, that we as Christians will reach the special place where we are able to "stand firm in all the will of God, mature and fully assured" (Col. 4:12).

In the Bible, one of the greatest examples of this transforming relationship is the life and ministry of the apostle Paul. Through a relationship of trust in God and Christ, Paul changed from a ruthless and relentless Christian persecutor into one of Christianity's loudest, boldest, and most persistent messengers. Even in the face of perplexing trials and physical hardship, Paul personally carried God's message of Christ throughout the world.

At the end of Paul's life, while chained to a wall in a Roman prison, he wrote a letter about his many trials and challenges. The letter was written to his beloved friend and protégé, pastor Timothy— "my son," Paul often affectionately called him. Paul's purpose in writing this letter was to encourage Timothy onward by sharing with him Paul's unwavering convictions about faith in God and Jesus Christ.

In the letter, Paul tells Timothy, "I was appointed a herald and an apostle and a teacher. That is why I am suffering as I am. Yet I am not ashamed, because I know whom I have believed, and am convinced that he is able to guard what I have entrusted to him for that day" (2 Tim. 1:11-12).

Paul goes on to tell Timothy:

> And the time has come for my departure. I have fought the good fight, I have finished the race, I have kept the faith. Now there is in store for me the crown of righteousness, which the Lord, the righteous Judge,

will award to me on that day—and not only to me, but also to all who have longed for his appearing. (2 Tim. 4:6-8)

Despite the immense trials and physical hardships he endured, and even knowing his death was close at hand, Paul was resolute and undeterred to the very end. He entrusted everything he had and everything he was to the Father and the Son, fully convinced that his trust was perfectly placed.

This was the great and final message of faith that Paul wanted to share with his dear friend Timothy. This was the faith—the trust—that Paul wanted Timothy to imitate and express in his own life.

King David's Trust

The Bible contains many other magnificent examples of the same deep and enduring faith. The Great Book is filled with the inspired stories of men and women who trusted God and, as a result, overcame impossible circumstances and achieved unimaginable dreams.

The life of King David is certainly one of these stories. In the book of Psalms, David left a marvelous record that describes the absolute and unshakable trust he had in God Almighty. In psalm after psalm, David details this faith that enabled him to grow from a simple shepherd boy into Israel's most cherished and acclaimed king.

Look at some of David's words that highlight his trust in God:

- In Psalm 62:7-8, David wrote, "My salvation and my honor depend on God; he is my mighty rock, my refuge. Trust in him at all times, O people; pour out your hearts to him, for God is our refuge."

- In Psalm 52:8, David professed, "I am like an olive tree flourishing in the house of God; I trust in God's unfailing love for ever and ever."

- In Psalm 32:10, David said, "Many are the woes of the wicked, but the Lord's unfailing love surrounds [the person] who trusts in him."

David trusted God with every fiber of his being. His psalms are filled with words of assurance, confidence, and conviction. Reading his psalms over and over has been one of my greatest joys and inspirations. Here was a person who, beyond all doubt, believed God would forever stand with him, in good times and in bad, and enable him to overcome every obstacle and enemy in his life.

In Psalm 31:14-15, David summed up his life of faith by declaring, "I trust in you, O Lord; I say, 'You are my God.' My times are in your hands."

RELATIONSHIPS BUILT ON TRUST

Both Paul and David understood it is essential to trust in God. Trusting God enabled Paul's successful ministry and allowed him to write about his confidence even while chained to a prison wall. Trusting God allowed David to enjoy countless victories and pen the many psalms chronicling God's strength and presence in his life. Trust was the foundation of it all.

And in the end, isn't that why trust is so fundamentally important to God and God's plans for each of us? It's trust that enables and sustains our relationship with him.

Think about it for a moment: What personal friendship, what marriage, what corporation or grouping of people can endure without trust? None. Not one. It's just not possible.

Where trust is absent, only paralysis, dysfunction, and fear result. The lifeblood of any relationship, group, or enterprise is and always will be trust. It's the substance that binds and the oil that lubricates so everything operates smoothly and efficiently.

Ask any management expert or successful business consultant who works with struggling corporations, and the issue of trust will always be underscored as a primary concern. It's a problem that tops the list for troubled and dysfunctional organizations.

To bring about the healthy and needed changes within these ailing organizations, trust must be reestablished within every layer of the organization. Mistrust ultimately infects everyone and everything. When employees lose "faith" in their leaders, managers, or coworkers, every aspect of the enterprise suffers and quickly turns negative.

Only trust can turn things around. As renowned management guru Peter F. Drucker indicated in the opening quote of our chapter, "Trust opens the door to change." In an environment of trust, people can and will change. In an environment of trust, functionality will return and creativity will reemerge.

Yes, trust opens the door to change, action, and interaction. Trust motivates men and women into new channels and positive directions. It supports accomplishment and inspires achievement. Trust is the ingredient that enables it all.

The same holds true for our relationship with God. Without faith—this secure trust in God—it's impossible for us to enter into a true and enduring relationship with him. Trust is the critical ingredient in our relationship with him.

To emphasize this point, we need only reflect on the troubling events that occurred when the early Israelites left Egypt on their way to the Promised Land. Despite all God had done to remove their yoke of slavery and despite his countless miracles as they traveled, many of the Israelites refused to trust in him.

Rather than put their trust in God, they grumbled and complained, saying, "Why is the Lord bringing us into this land only to let us fall by the sword? We should choose a leader and go back to Egypt" (Num. 14:3, 4).

Because of their lack of trust, the Israelites actually talked about retreating to Egypt and the brutal bonds of slavery.

In anger, the Lord said to Moses, "How long will these people treat me with contempt? How long will they refuse to believe in me, in spite of all the miraculous signs I have performed among them?" (Num. 14:11).

By not trusting God, they missed God's foundational message and glorious plan for their lives. From the Almighty's thundering voice, which literally shook Mount Sinai, to the signs and miracles he gave them with his own loving hand, none of this had lasting value for them.

"The message they heard was of no value to them because those who heard did not combine it with faith" is how the Bible describes the events and end result (Heb. 4:2).

No value. No benefit. Without giving over their hearts in trust to God, the Israelites never gained what God wanted them to have: an intimate and enduring relationship with him, the Creator, the one true God.

THE WEST VIRGINIA PREACHER

Perhaps one last example will so deeply drive home our central message of faith that we will never lose sight of it. The example comes from the life of Phil Donahue, the nationally acclaimed talk show host, and is delightfully detailed in the book *The Right Words at the Right Time* by his wife, Marlo Thomas.

I encourage everyone to search out a copy of this inspiring book and read the stories submitted by a wide array of people and personalities, each discussing a brief yet meaningful event that impacted their lives and careers.

In the forward to the book, Thomas describes the stories as "a brief glimpse into the heart, a moment of awakening, a light bulb that revealed a truth . . . or a challenge that moved them to action."

For Donahue, his moment of awakening grew out of a tense drama from his early career. Only twenty-seven years old at the time and a fledgling reporter for a local radio station in Ohio, Donahue had been assigned to cover a mine collapse in rural West Virginia. In this collapse, thirty-eight coal miners were trapped underground, and rescue efforts were desperately under way to save them.

As the rescue efforts escalated, the West Virginia mining accident captured increasing public attention. What was at first a regional story suddenly became a national story. The entire country wanted to be kept informed about the rescue.

With the growing interest in the story, CBS News contacted Donahue to ask whether he would deliver nightly radio reports on the rescue. Donahue, of course, jumped at the opportunity. For him, it was a major broadcasting assignment, one that would allow him to step into the national spotlight and perhaps advance his career.

Over the ensuing days, Donahue dutifully called in his reports to CBS News and his voice was heard across America. Each night, the country heard him describe the urgent efforts under way to save the trapped miners.

On the fourth day of the rescue, however, something even more unexpected happened for young Donahue: CBS News asked him to deliver a televised broadcast from the scene. It was yet another sea-change opportunity for him. No longer would it be Donahue's voice heard across America; now the country would see the young man himself as he broadcast his story. It was the big time for sure.

And Donahue knew exactly what he wanted to televise: As the families and townsfolk assembled with their local preacher to offer a unified prayer to God for help, Donahue signaled his TV cameraman to start filming. It was the perfect down-home, all-American scene.

It was so heartrending that Donahue began to conjure up images in his mind of the acclaim his broadcast might generate. What a scene! What a moment! What drama! A reporter simply couldn't envision a more moving moment for national TV coverage.

There was only one problem—one big problem: The camera wasn't working. In the cold night air, the camera had frozen and simply wouldn't run. Nothing was on celluloid; nothing had been preserved on film. Donahue had missed the big moment—his big moment—for all America to see.

As the cameraman shook his head in disbelief, Donahue scrambled for a solution. What to do? What to do?

There was only one solution: warm up the TV camera and ask the preacher to re-create the scene. Surely the preacher would be willing to act out the little drama again and get his chance at the national spotlight. Surely he would be pleased and eager to voice his prayer a second time and, who knows, perhaps even shed a small tear for national TV.

Of course, you know what happened next. Despite young Donahue's respectful requests and even some downright shameless begging, the preacher wouldn't do a second take for the camera.

"I have already prayed," he told Donahue. "It wouldn't be right. Wouldn't be honest. I have already prayed to my God." No amount of urging or arguments would change his mind.

For Donahue, the balloon had popped. His visions of acclaim and the national spotlight had vanished into the cold night sky.

For many months thereafter, Donahue remained unsettled as he pondered what had happened. Eventually, however, the realization dawned on him: In rural West Virginia, he had witnessed a most profound event, an event of genuine faith and true moral courage.

"In a world of posturing and religious pomp," Donahue would write, "here was a man of God who refused to perform for television. His prayer had already been offered and repeating it would have been phony."

It was an example of faith and courage that would forever impact Donahue's life and career as he went on to become one of America's most recognized and esteemed television personalities.

What a wonderful story! It captures the foundational message of faith perfectly. The West Virginia preacher, like all the great men and women of faith in the Bible, had a relationship of trust in his God, a relationship of trust that was sacred and genuine. He had prayed to "his God"—not someone else's God or some fuzzy conceptualization of God—for the lives of the miners trapped underground, and nothing would be allowed to overshadow or falsify that sacred bond.

The preacher's trust in God and the relationship that depended on it was all that mattered. It was what he had to be true to and what he was true to above all else.

Personal Reflections

Faith, at its core, is about trusting God.

My trust in God is what enables and sustains my personal relationship with him.

My trust in God opens the door to beneficial changes and leads me on a secure path for a strong, prosperous, and successful life.

2

God of His Word

"We trust not because 'a God' exists, but because 'this God' exists."

—*C. S. Lewis*

God takes his word seriously—and he must.

Think about the implications: How could you have a relationship of trust with "a god" who did not tell you the truth or who promised you one thing yet did another? It wouldn't be possible. No way. Period. End of story.

Stripped of the jargon, trust always comes down to saying what you mean and doing what you say. It's about the truthfulness of words and following through on promises. Without these elements, our ability to trust in an individual, a group, or even "a god" simply can't last.

TRUSTWORTHY WORDS

Thankfully, as C. S. Lewis points out in the opening quote of this chapter, we don't have "a god" but "this God"—a God of complete honesty and integrity. King David called him "the God of truth" and his words "right and true" (Ps. 31:5, 33:4). David said, "For the word of the Lord is right and true; he is faithful in all he does" (Ps. 33:4).

David used another valuable term to describe the words of God: trustworthy. I like that term because it's both personal and instructive. God's words to us are trustworthy; they are worthy of our trust. Worthy of a cherished place in our heart.

"O Sovereign Lord, you are God! Your words are trustworthy, and you have promised these good things to your servant," said David (2 Sam. 7:28).

Throughout the Bible, God affirms his message of uncompromising honesty and unequalled integrity. In the book of Isaiah, for example, God tells us in the clearest, most direct language possible, "What I have said, that will I bring about; what I have planned, that will I do" (Isa. 46:11).

God used the same direct language in the book of Numbers to tell us, "God is not a man that he should lie, nor a son of man, that he should change his mind. Does he speak and then not act? Does he promise and not fulfill?" (Num. 23:19).

For our benefit, God has declared over and over that he is a God of his word. What he speaks is never a lie. What he promises he always delivers. He never muddles his statements, couches his terms, or changes his mind. His words to us are trustworthy, right, and true.

In the gospels, Jesus often spoke about the honesty and integrity of God. For Jesus, one word best captured the flawless nature of God's promises to us: *truth*. "God's word is truth," said Jesus (John 17:17). It's the key term Jesus used most often whenever he spoke about his Father's integrity, wisdom, and promises for mankind.

The God of truth who brings us the word of truth: This is who and what we have available to help and guide us if we are willing to extend our trust in return.

In return for our trust, God has extended the truth about our wondrous journey on earth: why we're here, how he created us, and how we're supposed to live. He's extended the truth about his countless blessings and detailed plans to have us prosper. He's even extended the truth about the eternal life prepared for each of us when our earthly journey ends.

In exchange for our trust, God has offered men and women the truth about all of life. It's why believers around the world can, and so often do, refer to the collective verses of the Bible as "the Word." The Word, God's comprehensive truth for mankind. The Word, God's principles, plans, and precepts for each of us.

A PERFECT REFLECTION

If I could stress only one characteristic of God's Word to convey the significance that it holds for us, I would say God's Word is an extension of him. Whatever God is like, his Word is like. The resemblance is exact, down to the finest detail.

In Psalm 138, David addresses and beautifully captures this perfect harmony between God and his Word. In this psalm of praise, one of my favorites, David says:

> I will praise you, O Lord, with all my heart; before the "gods" I will sing your praise. I will bow down toward your holy temple and will praise your name for your love and your faithfulness, for you have exalted above all things your name and your word.
> (Ps. 138:1-2)

"For you have exalted above all things your name and your word": This is the assurance that highlights David's praise. Because of his love and faithfulness, God raised his Word and placed it on the highest pedestal possible—the same standard that defines who he is. There's no wiggle room or even the smallest discrepancy between the two. Who God is and what he says are in agreement, fully consistent in goodness, wisdom, and power.

This message, this standard, this relationship between God and his Word is profound. It's why, as David points out in Psalm 138, we can bow down and praise him, why we can worship him as holy. It's the reason we can trust God and believe everything he has promised us.

TIMELESS AND IMMOVABLE WORDS

The more we recognize and appreciate the flawless honesty and integrity that infuses every syllable of God's Word, the more certain and secure our trust becomes. So what else can we learn? What else can we come to understand?

In my own life, a major point of awakening came when I began to grasp the eternal and unchanging nature of God's promises.

Unlike man's always-changing statements, God's declarations are forever. They're not one thing today and another thing tomorrow. They don't deviate with the stock market or change course with public opinion. They don't depend on corporate bankers nor do they devalue over time.

God's words of wisdom and promise are eternal. They are forever relevant, vital, and pure—always illuminating, always guiding, always leading us to the very best for our life.

The apostle Peter, quoting from the book of Isaiah, spoke about the eternal quality of God's Word by telling us, "All men are like grass, and their glory is like the flowers of the field; the grass withers and the flowers fall, but the word of the Lord stands forever" (1 Peter 1:24-25).

Peter often called it "the living and enduring word of God" and its underlying truth an "imperishable seed" (1 Peter 1:23).

Jesus, teaching us about the unchanging nature of God's Word, said the same thing: "Heaven and earth will pass away, but my words will never pass away" (Matt. 24:35).

In Psalm 119, God's psalmist also pointed to the eternal nature of God's promises when he wrote, "Your word, O Lord, is eternal; it stands firm in the heavens. Your faithfulness continues through all generations; you established the earth, and it endures. Your laws endure to this day, for all things serve you" (Ps. 119:89-91).

Eternal, imperishable, unchanging, and forever true: these descriptors sum up the strength and timeless nature of God's truths. These truths are as alive, vibrant, and powerful today as they were when first spoken thousands of years ago. From the time of Adam's generation to the present, God's words of wisdom and promise remain certain and secure for each of us.

GOD-BREATHED WORDS

So where then do we find these special words? Where do we look for them?

The answer is straightforward: God has made them available to us by recording them in the Bible.

I know that sounds simplistic, but it is simple. God hasn't kept his promises to us a secret. He's written them down. In the Bible, we have a book given to us straight from the hand and the heart of God. It's the reason Paul routinely called the words of the Bible the Holy Scriptures.

Another term Paul often used when he described the Scriptures is "God breathed." They are words breathed, inspired, and prompted by God, not mankind's self-created stories, myths, and make-believe.

"All Scripture is God-breathed and is useful for teaching, rebuking, correcting, and training in righteousness, so that the [people] of God may be thoroughly equipped for every good work" (2 Tim. 3:16-17).

In his writings to the early church, Paul spoke of the great joy he experienced whenever this most important precept became a reality to believers. He wrote in 1 Thess. 2:13, "And we also thank God continually because, when you received the word of God, which you heard from us, you accepted it not as the word of men, but as it actually is, the word of God, which is at work in you who believe."

Paul stressed the phrase "as it actually is." God's Word, not our words. God's Word, not the philosophical musings of men and women. God's Word, not another version of so-called truth that people have dreamed up to peddle in the marketplace.

We've been given holy, divine, eternal declarations from the unlimited wisdom of God. They were given to work for us, with us, and in us—to benefit us in every way.

What an incredible asset we have to hold in our hands and nourish our lives. We literally have God's principles, plans, and promises laid out before us in detail—a compilation of thousands of years of

God's plan for mankind and God's workings on the earth. It's all there, written down to teach and guide us.

We may not have been with the Israelites on Mount Sinai when God's voice shook that mighty mountain. We may not have walked with Moses and the prophets when they issued the Lord's proclamations before the assembled crowds. We may not have been present when Jesus spoke to those in need and performed his many miracles. But we do have the tangible account of it all from God's own hand to enlighten us.

And just as importantly, we have God's promise that he will continue to perform these works and incredible miracles for us today if we will extend our trust to him.

The Word Made "Flesh"

In our discussions on the building blocks of faith, we've focused on the critical importance of our trust in God. To encourage and enable this trust, we've seen the seriousness God has placed in his Word, exalting it above all things as a perfect reflection of who he is and what he will do. There remains, however, one final building block of our faith.

What is this last block? It's our trust and acceptance of God's most beloved and illuminating word—what God calls the living Word, the Word made flesh. Yes, it's our trust and acceptance of the Lord Jesus Christ.

In the opening verses of the gospel of John, the Holy Spirit, through the hand of John, brings us this exquisite metaphor for Jesus as "the Word of God, the Word made flesh." It's one of the most striking metaphors in the Bible, one that has captured the hearts of believers since the words were first written millennia ago:

> In the beginning was the Word, and the Word was
> with God, and the Word was God. He was with God
> in the beginning. Through him all things were made;
> without him nothing was made that has been made.
> In him was life, and that life was the light of men.
> (John 1:1-4)

The Holy Spirit opens John's gospel in this way because this is where it all begins: God the Father and God the Son together throughout eternity. This is the truth of Jesus Christ, the reality of who he is.

"The Son is the radiance of God's glory and the exact representation of his being, sustaining all things by his powerful word" (Heb. 1:3). "He is the image of the invisible God, the firstborn over all creation" (Col. 1:15).

The opening verses of John's gospel continue God's message by telling of Jesus' coming in the body of a man to suffer as the final sacrifice for mankind's sins. His coming in this humble, fleshly form was the Father's ultimate plan, a plan that required immeasurable agony yet resulted in glory:

> The Word became flesh and made his dwelling
> among us. We have seen his glory, the glory of the
> One and Only, who came from the Father, full of
> grace and truth. (John 1:14)

The result of Jesus Christ's sacrifice and his return to his Father in glory was a gift beyond imaginable measure: our right to become the sons and daughters of God, the honored members of heaven's royal family! Of this unsurpassable gift, the Holy Spirit, through the pen of John, proclaims:

> He [Jesus Christ] was in the world, and though
> the world was made through him, the world did
> not recognize him. He came to that which was

his own, but his own did not receive him. Yet to all who received him, to those who believed in his name, he gave the right to become children of God—children born not of natural descent, nor of human decision or a husband's will, but born of God. (John 1:10-13)

In only a handful of sentences and through one exceptional metaphor, John's gospel testifies to the truth of Jesus Christ: his deity, his coming, his gift of service and sacrifice, and his return to glory. It's the central truth of Christianity and our ultimate trust in God. There is no firmer foundation for our faith. There is no other foundation for our faith.

"No one can lay any foundation other than the one already laid, which is Jesus Christ" (1 Cor. 3:11).

GOD'S GREATEST MESSAGE TO YOU

Every time we speak or write words on a page, those words become our instrument. They represent what we seek to express and convey to others. Said another way, those words are our agents, our representatives—servants of the speaker and the author.

In the same way, Jesus Christ—the Word of God, the Word made flesh—was God's instrument or agent when he came to earth. Commissioned by his Father and in the fleshly body of a man, Jesus came to fulfill God's plan of redemption for mankind. He didn't come cloaked in radiance and celestial majesty as King of kings; he came to us as a simple servant and sacrificial lamb.

Throughout the gospels, Jesus emphasized his obedient, earthly role to those who came to hear him speak:

- "For I have come down from heaven not to do my will but to do the will of him who sent me," said Jesus (John 6:38).

- "If God were your Father, you would love me," said Jesus to the assembled crowds, "for I came from God and now am here. I have not come on my own, but he sent me" (John 8:42-43).

- "For even the Son of Man did not come to be served, but to serve, and to give his life as a ransom for many," said Jesus to his disciples (Mark 10:45).

Even the specific words Jesus spoke while he walked the earth were a reflection of his role as servant and messenger for his Father. Jesus said to the people, "For I did not speak of my own accord, but the Father who sent me commanded me what to say and how to say it. I know that his command leads to eternal life. So whatever I say is just what the Father has told me to say" (John 12:49-50).

Jesus had no hidden agenda. His purpose on earth was to complete the work his Father asked him to accomplish and then return to the glory of heaven to remain forever at God's right hand, awaiting our joyful arrival. The words he spoke and the deeds he performed, even his final sacrifice on the cross, were those of a devoted servant.

In every conceivable way, Jesus Christ was God's perfect messenger and God's ultimate message for mankind. He truly was and, for all who will listen, continues to be the Word of God personified—the divine and eternal message of hope and love for all creation.

"In the past God spoke to our forefathers through the prophets at many times and in various ways, but in these last days he has spoken to us by his Son, whom he appointed heir of all things, and through whom he made the universe" (Heb. 1:1-2).

We must listen to the message of Jesus Christ and trust in him. As Jesus told each of us before his death on the cross, "Trust in God; trust also in me" (John 14:1).

Personal Reflections

Faith is about trusting God the Father and God the Son and believing their words, which were recorded for my benefit.

Their words to me are the genuine article—trustworthy, eternal, unchanging, and forever true.

3

Your Heart:
Uncovering the Wellspring of Life

"I love players with heart, not necessarily emotion, but those who deep down are driven by something more than mind and body."

—*Joe Torre*

"We need to become more spirit conscious. Spiritual things will become more real to us the more spirit conscious we become."

—*Kenneth E. Hagin*

Whenever we talk about trusting or believing, the word "heart" inevitably enters the discussion.

We talk about trusting people with our heart or believing their words and promises with all our heart. We wax on about our heart-held beliefs and the urge to follow our heart. We even point out that we're speaking from the heart when we want to emphasize the honest and sincere beliefs that accompany our words.

Yes, the heart—our heart—is always part of life's discussions. We can't avoid it. This word speaks to something basic and elemental within us. It somehow captures an unseen dimension inside each of us that reaches out for truth and guides our most important choices and decisions.

What's more remarkable about this special word is that everyone seems to understand what we mean whenever we use it. No one blinks an eye or gives us a funny look when we use it during a conversation. It's as if we each have an intuitive sense—a "words-can't-fully-describe-it" comprehension—of what it is.

It's not physical; it's not mental or intellectual either. "It's my heart, that's what it is. You know what I'm talking about. You know what I mean." That's pretty much how we as a society define it. Enough said. No one questions the concept further, and everyone nods in agreement.

But maybe there is more to it, more that you and I can do to define and understand this inner dimension that's so essential yet unseen. After all, if we're going to trust and believe with our heart and if we're going to follow and speak from it, a broader understanding would certainly be helpful.

In this chapter, let's see if we can put our finger more firmly on the pulse of this important element we call our heart.

A Greater Reality

"What will the kingdom look like? When will it come? Who will be a part of it?" the people asked Jesus.

Every Jew in Judea—Pharisees included—wanted to know the answers to these questions. They wanted to know when the promised kingdom of God would appear and trample the Roman

Empire and its tyrannical control over Jerusalem, Judea, and the rest of the known world.

They wanted to hear talk of God's armies, angelic hosts, and overwhelming might. They wanted to hear talk of great battles and even greater victories. In vivid detail, they wanted to learn about the coming of God's grand and glorious kingdom.

You could hear a pin drop as Jesus responded, "The kingdom of God is within you" (Luke 17:21).

What? That wasn't the answer the Jews were expecting to hear—or even wanted to hear. But Jesus needed them to understand another truth about God's kingdom, a preliminary and more pressing truth. He needed them to understand that the kingdom of God would be revealed within them first through a change on the inside—in their spirit.

This was God's plan first and foremost. Jesus had come to bring a new inner kingdom—the great and glorious spiritual kingdom of God—to all who would believe in him. God's external kingdom, with all its grandeur, would come but much later. It would come at the end of the age, a time known only to Father God. Not even Jesus knew the exact hour of its arrival (see Mark 13:32-33; Acts 1:6-7).

Nicodemus, a religious teacher, Pharisee, and highly regarded member of the Jewish ruling counsel, had similar questions for Jesus about the coming of God's kingdom. He, too, wanted to learn more about it. What would this kingdom look like? When would it come? Who would be part of it?

In response to Nicodemus' questions, Jesus answered him by saying, "I tell you the truth, no one can see the kingdom of God unless he is born again" (John 3:3).

Jesus' response baffled the scholarly Nicodemus. How could a man or woman be born again? Reenter a mother's womb and be born a second time? How? It just wasn't possible.

Knowing Nicodemus' puzzlement, Jesus clarified his words. He was speaking to Nicodemus about heavenly reality, spiritual reality—an eternal world that was invisible to the naked eye yet was just as real, more real in fact. This was the enduring understanding of life and creation to which Jesus was pointing Nicodemus.

The answers Nicodemus was searching for couldn't and wouldn't be found in the natural world of his physical senses. Only God's spiritual reality with God's gift of spiritual rebirth held these answers. To see, experience, and be part of God's kingdom, Nicodemus would need to be born again on the inside by the power of God's Holy Spirit. A physical rebirth would change nothing; a spiritual rebirth would change everything.

Jesus described it like this to Nicodemus:

> I tell you the truth, no one can enter the kingdom of God unless he is born of water and the Spirit. Flesh gives birth to flesh, but the Spirit gives birth to spirit. You should not be surprised at my saying, "You must be born again." The wind blows wherever it pleases. You hear its sound but you cannot tell where it comes from or where it is going. So it is with everyone born of the Spirit. (John 3:5-8)

The lessons for Nicodemus are, of course, our lessons as well. To fully grasp the miracle that is our life, we must expand our understanding of it by looking beyond the natural world.

What we see with our eyes, what we touch with our hands, and what we interpret with our senses is not the complete reality of life, the universe, or God's creation. There is more, much more. God's infinite power, creativity, and breadth of insight stretch far beyond the limits of our earthly senses and our temporal world.

A temporal world sees only a corruptible planet filled with men and women who live limited, temporary lives. A natural world sees only bodies of flesh and a humanity with little to gain. A spiritual world, however, sees the opposite. It sees a brilliant, boundless, limitless world filled with unique and extraordinary spiritual beings. It sees an unending universe created by a loving God for men and women to enjoy and appreciate forever. It sees a life for each of us that is truly life without end.

God has given us the miracle of life, but to understand and appreciate this gift, you and I must focus our attention on God's greater reality. To use a term coined by the Rev. Kenneth E. Hagin, we need to become more "spirit conscious." As we become more aware of our own spiritual nature and God's spiritual world, the gifts and workings of God and his kingdom will become more real to us.

"Spiritual things will become more real to us, the more spirit conscious we become," stressed Hagin throughout his ministry and in his teachings on faith.

God has a greater reality for us, both today and tomorrow—a reality that centers on the spiritual, the supernatural, the eternal. To grow and change, we must refocus on this infinite world that's there just beyond our earthly senses.

As Paul explained, "We fix our eyes not on what is seen, but on what is unseen. For what is seen is temporary, but what is unseen is eternal" (2 Cor. 4:18).

The Real "You"

The unseen realm—the spiritual realm—holds the key to who we are. Despite our physical appearance, we are not temporary beings who exist for only a moment in time and then vanish into the ether, never to be seen or heard from again. Quite the contrary, we are eternal, spiritual beings who, for our limited time on earth, inhabit a perishable body.

In chapter 12 of the gospel of Luke, Jesus said much about our eternal existence.

Speaking to his disciples and the assembled crowds, Jesus explained the perishable nature of the human body but the imperishable nature of mankind. Jesus wanted everyone to understand and carefully consider the reality of his or her existence, an existence that vastly overshadows our momentary time here on earth. He also wanted people to understand that our eternal future is under God's ultimate power and control.

"I tell you, my friends, do not be afraid of those who kill the body and after that can do no more," Jesus told them. "But I will show you whom you should fear: Fear him who, after the killing of the body, has power to throw you into hell. Yes, I tell you, fear him" (Luke 12:4-5).

The real you—the eternal you—is the spiritual person who will continue to live on long after your body has died. Your body is only your temporary covering. Your core, your essence, your innermost self is spirit, not flesh.

I like what Peter and Paul often called our natural bodies: earthly tents.

"I think it is right to refresh your memory as long as I live in the tent of this body," wrote Peter, "because I know that I will soon

34

put it aside as our Lord Jesus Christ has made clear to me" (2 Peter 1:13-14).

It's only inside our tent that our true life and eternal nature is found. One day, each of us will leave this temporary and fragile shelter. We will continue on to a new place, our heavenly place with God the Father and God the Son.

At that time, you and I will be given a new and imperishable body to house our imperishable spirit. It will be like the body given to Jesus Christ when God raised him from the dead. A body that doesn't age, deteriorate, or falter. A body that is as blessed and eternal as we are.

Paul wrote, "Now we know that if the earthly tent we live in is destroyed, we have a building from God, an eternal house in heaven not built by human hands" (2 Cor. 5:1).

The real you, the real me—we are spirit beings who inhabit eternity. This is how the Lord "who forms the spirit of man within him" (Zech. 12:1) made each of us and placed us at the center of his creative plan.

Your Spiritual "Heart"

By comparing our bodies to a tent or temporary covering, we have a wonderful image to help us understand the temporary condition of the human body. But what about our spirit? Is there a word or an image that captures our inner dimension, our spiritual dimension?

There is. It's the special word we talked about earlier, the one we routinely employ in life's discussions: heart. Throughout the Bible—and most especially the New Testament—the heart is the primary image or metaphor used to describe our spiritual dimension.

Let's look at a few brief Scripture passages to understand how this metaphorical word is used in biblical contexts:

In the book of Corinthians, Paul used the heart to describe the abiding presence of God's Holy Spirit within our spirit whenever we accept Jesus Christ as our Lord and Savior.

Paul said, "You show that you are a letter from Christ, the result of our ministry, written not with ink but with the Spirit of the living God, not on tablets of stone but on tablets of human hearts" (2 Cor. 3:3).

In Galatians, Paul wrote about the heart as our innermost dimension and the place where the Holy Spirit confirms for us our new birth and inheritance as sons and daughters of God.

Paul said, "Because you are [sons and daughters], God sent the Spirit of his Son into our hearts, the Spirit who calls out Abba, Father" (Gal. 4:6).

Peter also used the heart as his model when he taught about our spiritual rebirth. Through the gospel of Christ and the power of the Holy Spirit, God's gift of spiritual rebirth—what Peter called a purified heart—became available to everyone, both Jew and Gentile:

> You know that some time ago God made a choice among you that the Gentiles might hear from my lips the message of the gospel and believe. God, who knows the heart, showed that he accepted them by giving the Holy Spirit to them, just as he did to us. He made no distinction between us and them, for he purified their hearts by faith. (Acts 15:7-9)

The heart was also Peter's model when he urged us to focus on the innermost aspect of who we are. He wrote, "Let it be the hidden person of the heart, with the imperishable quality of a gentle and quiet spirit, which is precious in the sight of God" (1 Peter 3:4 NASB).

Peter understood that it's not our physical appearance that matters most to God but our inward self—"the hidden person of the heart."

THE HEART'S REFLECTION

From the book of Proverbs, let's look at one last Scripture on this metaphor of the heart. In only twelve words, Prov. 27:19 offers us one of the most perceptive looks at this symbolism by telling us, "As water reflects a face, so a man's heart reflects the man."

These words from Proverbs are actually a metaphor wrapped within an analogy. Let me help you unravel the meaning through some simple paraphrasing:

> A mirror of calm water reflects and reveals your face or outward appearance, but it's your heart that reflects and reveals your inner essence—the real man or woman you are.

According to Proverbs, God's Book of Wisdom, who you are is not a reflection of your outward physical body but a reflection of your inward spirit, your heart. It's your heart that best defines you. It's your heart that makes you who you are.

Doesn't this symbolism ring true? What better way to describe our innermost dimension that's so vital yet unseen? In one small word, so much meaning and importance is conveyed about how God created us. It gets to the very heart of the matter.

Once, when asked what he looked for in a professional athlete, Joe Torre, the renowned Major League Baseball manager, said, "I love players with heart, not necessarily emotion, but those who deep down are driven by something more than mind and body."

For Torre, it wasn't physical stature, mental acuity, or other outward factors often heralded by the media that impressed him most. What impressed him was a player's heart. That's what made the greatest difference; that's what distinguished the good from the great. With one small word—heart—Torre put his finger on what mattered most.

This small word also reveals why we as human beings have always been consumed by the spectacle of athletic competition in its many forms. Through these contests and competitions, especially at the world-class level, we put a spotlight on the three dimensions of every man and woman: spirit, mind, and body.

In these competitions, we see the astonishing strength and endurance of the human body. We see the remarkable focus, perception, and split-second reactions of the human mind. More importantly, we see the commanding element that inspires and enables it all: the incomparable human spirit, the eternal heart, the heart of a champion.

FAITH IS OF THE HEART

But why is this word important for this book, and why have I spent so much time laying a foundation about the heart? Isn't this a book about faith and faith's expressions?

Well, the answer is quite simple: Faith is of the heart. That's the dimension where faith lives and breathes, grows and speaks.

In our heart, we reach out to trust God. In our heart, we grab hold of God's words and allow them to become part of who we are on the inside. With our heart and from our heart, we embrace and express all that God has promised us.

Our journey of faith isn't about how smart we are, how photographic our memories are, or how big and brawny our cerebral cortexes may be. Faith is not an intellectual exercise to be scored or a mental test to be passed. It's not "mind over matter" or some form of transcendental task.

Having faith is about the role and function of our spirit together with the help of the Holy Spirit. Deep within us, our heart is actively and purposefully engaged as we trust God and believe his many promises.

Rom. 10:10 confirms this point by declaring that "it is with your heart that you believe."

"Trust in the Lord with all your heart and lean not on your own understanding" is how Prov. 3:5 makes the point.

And in Ps. 28:7, David counsels us on the role of our heart in faith by explaining that "my heart trusts in him and I am helped."

Jesus also confirms our understanding in Mark 11:23 when he teaches about the words of faith that come from the heart. Here he tells us "not to doubt in [our] heart but believe" in order to speak the words that bring God's supernatural results.

The more we reflect on the heart's role in faith, doesn't it make sense? God isn't looking for a college degree or an IQ score for his truths to resonate within us and be accepted by us. God, who knows the heart, looks to our heart and speaks to it.

"For the Lord seeth not as man seeth; for man looketh on the outward appearance, but the Lord looketh on the heart" (1 Sam. 16:7 KJV).

The heart—your heart—is where the inner conviction, the certainty, the knowing-that-you-know takes root and grows. The heart—your heart—is where you recognize and accept God's spiritual truths. Our mind can take us only so far on this journey; the ultimate step—the step of faith—comes from the heart.

I like the way Billy Graham often made the distinction between spiritual faith and intellectual knowledge: "You cannot come to Christ with just your mind," he said. "You can't think your way to Jesus."

The decision to trust and accept Jesus Christ is a decision of the heart—a spiritual decision. Sure, your mind and your intellect hear (and must hear) the message of Christ, but it's from your heart that the trust must ultimately come.

"Head knowledge" vs. "heart faith" is another way to draw this important distinction. Just because we know something intellectually doesn't mean we believe it as a living truth in our heart. Just because we've memorized a Bible passage doesn't mean we've grabbed hold of it for our life.

In our head, we know and understand many ideas and concepts. And that's certainly an important and necessary part of successful living, especially in today's information age. But knowing something—for example, knowing what a light switch is and how it works—isn't the same as actually turning that light switch on.

It's no different with faith. Our mind helps us hear and understand the words of God's message, but our mind can't do it all. It can't turn the words into truth; it can't turn on the critical switch.

To trust God and accept his words as truth, your heart must flip that switch. Your heart must complete the circuit. When that happens, a marvelous light beams brightly within you, illuminating your path and guiding your steps.

In the Bible, we often see the men and women of the early church demonstrating this heart-centered response of faith. For example, in the second chapter of Acts, Peter preached the gospel of Christ to a crowd of thousands in Jerusalem on the day of Pentecost, and more than three thousand people believed his message.

Acts 2:37 describes their response to Peter's message by telling us, "They were cut to the heart."

The message registered in their spirit! On the inside, in the depths of their heart, they believed and accepted God's word as truth. It wasn't merely an intellectual experience for these men and women; it was a spiritual experience.

YOUR LIFE-GIVING RESERVOIR

The Bible gives us many wonderful pictures and images from everyday life to help us understand spiritual principles and spiritual workings. After all, a picture does speak a thousand words.

And that's certainly true of another colorful image God has given us to better understand the role of our heart. The image is that of a dynamic reservoir, one that stores and keeps our most valuable, life-forming, and life-supporting resources. It's a picture that emphasizes our need to internalize God's Word within us so those truths can be brought forth and released into our life.

We see this image taught by Jesus in chapter 6 of Luke's gospel. Here Jesus compares our heart to a storehouse, and he tells us that "the good man brings good things out of the good stored up in his heart" (Luke 6:45). The King James Version uses the word "treasure" in place of the word "things." I like that: The good person brings out the "good treasure" he or she has stored in his or her heart.

In the parable of the sower from Luke chapter 8, Jesus draws a similar picture when he tells his disciples that "the seed is the word of God" and the soil where it grows is "the heart" (Luke 8:11-15).

In the rich soil of our heart, Jesus says, is where we each must plant and grow God's Word so it becomes a harvestable product to nourish our life. The seed requires the soil for the harvest to come.

Proverbs uses even more colorful imagery by comparing our heart to a wellspring—a wellspring of life: "Above all else, guard your heart, for it is the wellspring of life" (Prov. 4:23).

Think about that picture for a moment: Your heart is the precious spring that feeds your life. It's what holds and carries your cherished beliefs, prized values, and deepest desires. It's what collects and carries the people you dearly trust, the words and promises you genuinely believe, and the things you treasure most. It's a collection, combination, and pooling together of these elements that make you who you are.

From this vital spring flow the issues of your life—the beliefs, precepts, and standards you look to for support and nourishment. From this spring come your wisdom, insights, attitude, and intentions. It's the source that inspires your thinking, motivates your actions, and fuels your dreams. When you give from it and speak from it, you express to the world around you all the things you fervently believe in and want to share.

If God's Word—his truth—isn't part of your spring, what becomes of your life? Aren't you crippled? Aren't you headed for constant trouble and wrong decisions?

Isn't this why the Bible pleads with us over and over to internalize God's Word so it becomes part of us, part of our life-giving well? Isn't this why God, in the book of Proverbs, repeatedly tells us:

- "store up my commands within you" (Prov. 2:1; 7:1);
- "write them on the tablet of your heart" (Prov. 7:3);
- "keep my commands in your heart" (Prov. 3:1);
- "lay hold of my words with all your heart" (Prov. 4:4);
- "bind them on your heart forever" (Prov. 6:21).

I know for me it's the reason the words of Proverbs 22 are always before my eyes, guiding and reminding me:

> Pay attention and listen to the sayings of the wise;
> apply your heart to what I teach, for it is pleasing
> when you keep them in your heart and have all of
> them ready on your lips. (Prov. 22:17-18)

Jesus emphasized this same message for us when he said, "All things are possible to [those] who believe" (Mark 9:23 NASB).

If we want God's changes in our life, if we want to benefit and grow, if we want to take our life to the next level of maturity and insight, we must apply God's Word to our heart. With God's Word as our wisdom, we become unstoppable. With God's Word as our trusted guide, we can achieve the impossible and enrich the world around us.

THE SPIRIT OF TRUTH

When it comes to trusting God and believing his Word, remember that you're never alone on this spiritual journey of faith.

Neither God nor Christ has sent you off alone to somehow find your way, to stumble on the truth. You've been given a helper, a divine counselor—someone whom Jesus rightly calls "the Spirit of truth"—to help and guide you.

"And I will ask the Father, and he will give you another Counselor to be with you forever—the Spirit of truth," said Jesus (John 14:16-17).

As promised, the Spirit of truth is with us today, alive and well, moving on the earth and living in the heart of every believer. All day, every day, this Spirit works for us and ministers to us, gently urging and counseling us on the inside.

Deep within, this Spirit whispers for us to accept as truth the words in the Bible. If you listen closely, you can hear this counselor even now, tugging on your heart, quietly saying, "Yes, the words are truth. Yes, it's OK to trust. Yes, please believe the words of the Bible, as they are God's promises to you."

What is this Spirit of truth that's guiding us? It is, of course, the Holy Spirit.

One of the Holy Spirit's most important roles is to help each of us unlock the truth of God's Word. Instead of being a fictional story, a pleasant myth, or an intellectual concept, the Holy Spirit encourages us to accept the words of the Bible as much more. His goal is to help us embrace the Scriptures as a tangible, living truth that our heart can confidently take in without fear of foolishness or deception.

In his letters to the early churches, Paul highlighted this role of the Holy Spirit in our life. Paul explained that God's words are spiritual truths to be grasped on the inside, in our spirit, with the help of the Holy Spirit.

He explained it like this:

> We have not received the spirit of the world but the Spirit who is from God, that we may understand what God has freely given us. This is what we speak, not in words taught us by human wisdom but in

words taught us by the Spirit, expressing spiritual truths in spiritual words. (1 Cor. 2:12-13)

Paul explained that without the Holy Spirit to help us, so much of God's wisdom would remain hidden in a cloak of foolishness. Men and women "without the Spirit [do] not accept the things that come from the Spirit of God, for they are foolishness to [them]," Paul said in 1 Cor. 2:14.

As a Christian, you have the spirit of God—the Spirit of truth—living in your heart. It's an inseparable presence, one that connects you forever to the Father and the Son and their heavenly kingdom. The Spirit of truth is your gift, part of your inheritance, and a confirmation of your new life.

If you will listen to the Holy Spirit's gentle prompting, he will lead you to truth in every area of your life. If you will listen, he will even reveal to you events that have yet to unfold in your life. "When he, the Spirit of truth, comes he will guide you into all truth . . . and he will tell you what is yet to come" (John 16:13).

Personal Reflections

I am an eternal, spiritual being who will live on long after my temporary, fleshly body has been buried in the earth.

With my heart—my innermost self—I reach out to trust God and believe his many promises.

The Holy Spirit—the Spirit of truth—is here to help me as I step out to embrace God's Word as the truth for my life, a living truth to guide, nourish, and inspire me.

4

How to Fill Your Heart
with God's Word: Six Steps

"Make the most of yourself by fanning the tiny, inner sparks of possibility into flames of achievement."
— *Golda Meir*

"Spectacular achievement is always preceded by unspectacular preparation."
— *Robert Schuller*

Jesus inspired us with profound wisdom when he told us that "all things are possible" for those who believe God's promises (Mark 9:23). Not some things, many things, or even most things—but all things! That's a lot of things, and that certainly covers everything we may ever need or face in life.

But how do we encourage our hearts to believe this?

This chapter outlines six steps to help you get started. By following these steps for internalizing God's Word, your efforts will be rewarded with rich and meaningful results.

STEP 1: PAYING ATTENTION

The primary way we fill our heart with God's Word is through study and focus—by paying attention. With your eyes and your ears and through the channel of your mind, you give your spirit access to God's promises. Your eyes, ears, and focused mind are the door to your heart.

Look again at the verses of Proverbs 22, where God instructs us to pay attention in order to apply his Word to our heart: "Pay attention and listen to the sayings of the wise; apply your heart to what I teach, for it is pleasing when you keep them in your heart and have all of them ready on your lips. So that your trust may be in the Lord, I teach you today, even you" (Prov. 22:17-19).

The emphasis on our need for study and focus is also brought out in Proverbs 4. In clear and emphatic terms, God tells us:

> Pay attention to what I say; listen closely to my words.
> Do not let them out of your sight, keep them within
> your heart; for they are life to those who find them
> and health to [your] whole body. (Prov. 4:20-22)

It's the same instruction Paul gave to Timothy when he was preparing Timothy to lead the early church at Ephesus. Paul told him: "Study and be eager and do your utmost to present yourself to God . . . a workman who has no cause to be ashamed, correctly analyzing and accurately dividing—rightfully handling and skillfully teaching—the Word of Truth" (2 Tim. 2:15 AMP).

Study, pay attention, focus, don't let the words out of your sight: This is how we apply God's Word to our heart. This is how we open the door to our spiritual wellspring and store God's truths within us.

Unfortunately, there's no way around this work of study and preparation. It doesn't happen by osmosis. We must give our heart a message to feed on, to grab hold of, to translate into truth. Our heart simply can't believe what we haven't heard, what we haven't read, what we haven't been taught or exposed to in God's Word.

Paul stressed this critical point to believers by saying, "So then faith cometh by hearing, and hearing by the word of God" (Rom. 10:17 KJV).

Alexander Hamilton, one of the United States' founding fathers and a great innovator, often emphasized a similar message about our need for study and focus.

Whenever his admiring public would view his accomplishments and attempt to label him a genius, Hamilton would quickly respond to them by saying:

> Men give me credit for genius, but all the genius
> I have lies in this: When I have a subject in mind,
> I study it profoundly. Day and night it is before
> me . . . The result is what some people call the fruits
> of genius, whereas it is in reality the fruits of study
> and labor.

Set aside time each week to study God's Word. Go through your weekly calendar and schedule the time, just as you would for all your important appointments. Make your time in God's Word a top priority for your life. Give God's Word the close attention it requires and deserves.

STEP 2: MEDITATION

When the Lord was preparing Joshua to become Israel's leader after Moses' death, his instructions were as follows: "This book of the law shall not depart out of your mouth, but you shall meditate on it day and night, that you may observe and do according to all that is written in it; for then you shall make your way prosperous, and then you shall deal wisely and have good success" (Josh. 1:8 AMP).

"Keep meditating on my Word" is a key part of what God was emphasizing to Joshua. Keep meditating so my Word fills your heart and continually flows from your mouth. Keep meditating so my principles, plans, and precepts are always an essential part of who you are and what you do.

If Joshua would do this, stressed God, then his path would be clear, his dealings wise, and his life both prosperous and successful.

The Lord's instructions were not intended for Joshua alone but for us as well. We, too, are to keep meditating on God's Word so it fills our heart, overflows from our mouth, and remains an essential part of who we are and what we do. But how? What is this practice we call meditation?

Meditation is simply the process of rolling God's words over and over in our mind so our thoughts can remain focused on them. Perhaps more plainly, we could call meditation the process of focused reflection or quiet repetition because that's what we're doing: We're replaying over and over in our mind the Scriptures we want to grasp, absorb, and embrace for our life.

In many ways, the meditation process is no different than the thought process we follow when we worry or fret over what someone may have said to us or about us. We replay and rehash those words over and over again. The only difference—and it's a big one—is that worrying is a debilitating and destructive process, whereas meditating on God's Word is a nourishing and constructive one.

Here's how to begin: Start by setting aside just ten minutes each day to quietly reflect on one Scripture. Ten minutes, one Scripture— that's it.

Now get comfortable. Sit or lie down. Then close your eyes and begin to repeat the words of that Scripture in your mind. Softly mutter the words aloud to yourself as you repeat them in your mind. The goal is to keep your thoughts fully focused on the words of that Scripture. Sound easy? It is easy! But it will require your commitment.

Psychologists have a special word for the repetitive thought process: rumination. The term comes from the digestive process of cows and other animals that digest their food by first forming it into a cud and then chewing that cud repeatedly to allow digestion to occur.

For ruminating animals, it's not a quick one-step process of consumption but rather a slow and repetitive practice that breaks down the nutrients in their food, allowing the nutrients to be fully absorbed and assimilated.

Absorption through rumination is what meditation is all about. By allowing your mind to contemplate again and again the words of God—to slowly "chew" them over and over—you are digesting and taking in those vital words of nourishment, making them an integral part of who you are on the inside. It's what the prophet Jeremiah remarked before God when he said, "When your words came I ate them; they were my joy and my heart's delight" (Jer. 15:16).

Finally, also look at the verses of Psalm 119 where God's psalmist highlights meditation more than seven different times, elevating the practice as one praiseworthy before God:

- "Oh, how I love your law! I meditate on it all day long," he announced to the Lord (v. 97).

- "I lift up my hands to your commands, which I love, and I meditate on your decrees," he confided (v. 48).

- The psalmist even goes so far as to say before God, "I have more insight than all my teachers, for I meditate on your statutes" (v. 99).

Take the time to start meditating. Make this invaluable commitment. It will strengthen and embolden your faith life.

STEP 3: VERBALIZE TO INTERNALIZE

One of the best ways to internalize God's Word is to externalize it. Yes, the more we outwardly verbalize the words of God, the more readily those words become internalized in our heart.

I know this may sound strange or even eccentric. But think about the concept for a moment: Through the process of verbalization, God's words literally become our spoken words. We recite them, become engaged in the speaking and the listening—and begin to take ownership. And the more we verbalize those words, the greater our ownership in them becomes.

The Bible confirms the benefits. Go back again to what God told us about how faith comes: "Faith cometh by hearing, and hearing by the word of God" (Rom. 10:17 KJV).

Just as we hear God's words played in the chambers of our mind during study and meditation, we hear the words again distinctly through our own speaking. Our own voice broadcasts God's message so our heart can listen and feed upon this truth.

Paul taught the benefits of verbalizing God's Word in many of his letters to early believers. In Colossians 3:16, Paul wrote, "Let the word of Christ dwell in you richly as you teach and admonish one another with all wisdom, and as you sing psalms, hymns and spiritual songs with gratitude in your hearts to God."

In Philemon 1:6, Paul also said, "I pray that you may be active in sharing your faith, so that you will have a full understanding of every good thing we have in Christ."

By sharing God's Word with others and by offering it up to the Lord in psalms, hymns, and spiritual songs, we allow God's Word to dwell in us richly. By sharing and verbalizing, we increase our understanding of every good thing we have in Christ. It works!

Perhaps no one was more adamant about the benefits of verbalizing God's Word through psalms, hymns, and spiritual songs than Martin Luther, the sixteenth-century theologian.

Luther, a skilled musician from childhood, penned more than thirty-five hymns in his lifetime, all with the purpose of helping Christians internalize God's promises while at the same time giving praise to God. "I wish to compose sacred hymns so that the word of God may dwell among the people also by means of song," wrote Luther.

Here's a great way to begin verbalizing God's Word: Write down one or two Scriptures you want to own for your life. Then in the bathroom mirror, in your car, at your desk—wherever you can—start speaking those Scriptures out loud to yourself. But don't stop there. Discuss, teach, and share those Scriptures with others.

While you're at it, find psalms, hymns, and spiritual songs that magnify these same truths of God. Or if music is one of your gifts, create your own songs. Sing them at home, in church, or with friends.

Have fun and enjoy the process. Verbalize all that you want to internalize!

Step 4: Prayer

There's nothing like prayer. It's essential to everything in the Christian life. When it comes to internalizing God's Word, it's no less essential.

James reminded us of this fact when he said, "If any of you lacks wisdom, he should ask God, who gives generously to all without finding fault, and it will be given to him" (James 1:5).

Jesus also told us to ask in prayer for growth and spiritual insight. He gave us these reliable instructions: "Ask and it will be given to you; seek and you will find; knock and the door will be opened to you. For everyone who asks receives; he who seeks finds; and to him who knocks, the door will be opened" (Matt. 7:7-8).

Some of my favorite prayers for spiritual growth come from Psalm 119, which chronicles one man's unrelenting quest to internalize God's teachings in the Scriptures. I encourage you to read this psalm in its entirety in order to grasp this person's voracious hunger for understanding and insight. This psalm will make you think deeply about your own life and the wisdom you're searching for.

Let me highlight four short prayers from Psalm 119, prayers you can begin praying today for your own growth and spiritual insight:

- "Lord, open my eyes that I may see wonderful things in your law" (v. 18).

- "Lord, your hands made me and formed me; give me understanding to learn your commands" (v. 73).

- "Lord, deal with your servant according to your love and teach me your decrees. I am your servant; give me discernment that I may understand your statutes" (vv. 124-125).

- "May my cry come before you, O Lord; give me understanding according to your word" (v. 169).

When accompanied with our sincerity, commitment, and trust, these are the prayers God longs to answer for us. These are the same prayers God longs to answer for our families, friends, and communities as well.

Let me share one additional prayer that you can begin praying today for your spiritual growth. This prayer was given to Paul by the Holy Spirit and is highlighted in Paul's letter to the church at Ephesus. It's a prayer I've prayed thousands of times for my own life and as an integral part of my ministry.

In his letter, Paul tells of praying this prayer for those who were members of the early church. If, however, we change Paul's wording from third person to first person (from "you" to "me"), this prayer becomes our own personal request before God:

> Glorious Father, I ask you, the God of my Lord Jesus Christ, to give me the Spirit of wisdom and revelation, so that I may know you better.
>
> I pray also that the eyes of my heart may be enlightened in order that I may know the hope to which you have called me; the riches of your glorious inheritance in the saints; and your incomparably great power for us who believe.
>
> That power is like the working of your mighty strength, which you exerted in Christ when you raised him from the dead and seated him at your right hand in the heavenly realms, far above all rule and authority, power and dominion, and every title that can be given, not only in the present age but also in the one to come.

> And Father God, you placed all things under his feet
> and appointed him to be head over everything for the
> church, which is his body, the fullness of him who
> fills everything in every way. (Eph. 1:17-23)

I urge you to begin praying Paul's prayer regularly for yourself and
for others. If you pray, you will experience God's spirit working to
unfold great wisdom and revelation in your life and in the lives of
others.

STEP 5: WALKING IN THE LIGHT YOU ALREADY HAVE

The more willing and committed we are to walk in the light we
already possess, the brighter our light will become. "The path of the
righteous is like the first gleam of dawn, shining ever brighter till
the full light of day," declares Prov. 4:18.

Jesus guided us on this same walk when he said, "Consider
carefully what you hear. With the measure you use, it will be
measured to you—and even more. Whoever has will be given
more" (Mark 4:24-25).

In Psalm 119, God's psalmist also emphasized this bright path for us
to follow when he declared before God, "I have considered my ways
and have turned my steps to your statutes" (v. 59). He promised God
that his heart was set on walking in this light always—"to the very
end" (v. 112).

If you will do what you know God has already asked you to do, many
of your problems and concerns will instantly fall to the wayside. It's
through willingness and commitment that we move forward, grow,
and experience the full advancement we desire in life.

STEP 6: EMBRACE GOD'S WORD AS YOUR TREASURE

If we could symbolize or personify God's Word in the image of a trusted woman, what would she say to us? How would she guide us? What fascinating qualities would we learn about her?

Perhaps she would say:

> I love those who love me, and those who seek me find me. With me are riches and honor, enduring wealth and prosperity.
>
> My fruit is better than fine gold; what I yield surpasses choice silver. I walk in the way of righteousness, along the paths of justice, bestowing wealth on those who love me and making their treasuries full. (Prov. 8:17-21)

Or perhaps she would point out to us:

> Do not forsake wisdom, and she will protect you; love her, and she will watch over you.
>
> Esteem her, and she will exalt you; embrace her, and she will honor you. (Prov. 4:6, 8)

Then again, maybe this is what we would learn about her:

> She is more precious than rubies; nothing you desire can compare with her. Long life is in her right hand; in her left hand are riches and honor.
>
> Her ways are pleasant ways and all her paths are peace. She is a tree of life to those who embrace her; those who lay hold of her will be blessed. (Prov. 3:15-18)

I know you get the point, but this counsel is indispensable for your life and success. In these words and images, God leads and guides us to envision and embrace his Word for the priceless and incomparable treasure that "she" most certainly is for our lives. He wants us to capture this understanding of his truth, reflect on it continually, and lay hold of its riches with the overwhelming desire of our heart.

By treasuring God's Word in your mind and heart, you will have what God wants you to have and become what God wants you to become.

Grab hold of this vision—the priceless treasure of God's Word. Keep it as your life's goal and passion. The rewards are limitless.

THE HEARTFELT WORDS OF THOMAS CLARKSON

Near London stands a monument to a man whose words captured the heart of a nation and whose story is both inspiring and instructional: Thomas Clarkson. It's a story about how words, once internalized by the heart, can change things forever—change a life, a mission, an injustice, a nation.

Let me share Clarkson's remarkable story, which highlights much of what we've learned in Part I of this book.

In 1785, Thomas Clarkson, a twenty-five-year-old Cambridge student, decided to enter the university's annual Latin essay contest. The yearly contest, with its coveted prize, was an intellectual challenge pursued by the brightest minds in England. To win such a prestigious competition was to earn a young man many accolades and even advance his career.

The topic for Cambridge's competition that year was one of the times: *Anne liceat invitos in servitutem dare*—Is it lawful to enslave the unconsenting? Yes, the essay was to be about slavery.

The university's vice chancellor, who had chosen the subject, was troubled by the appalling apathy and indifference of Britain's judicial system to the burgeoning British slave trade and its horrific toll on human life and dignity. He hoped this essay topic would raise critical questions.

Like most, Clarkson hadn't thought much about slavery up to that point in his life. There was certainly much for him to learn. He would need to read, study, and research; he would need to find out for himself what slavery was really all about.

After extensive and detailed research, including many personal interviews and long nights of study, Clarkson wrote his essay. It won first prize!

Clarkson was thrilled, as was the entire Cambridge community. Both students and faculty congratulated him on his intellectual efforts and his scholarly prize. The accolades and recognition were exhilarating for young Clarkson.

But Clarkson's life was about to change in other more significant ways.

The change began in his thought life. Day after day, Clarkson replayed the words of his essay in his mind. He couldn't get away from those words—the appalling injustice, inhumane conditions, outright murder. The words were constantly before him. They challenged him at every turn.

As Clarkson contemplated what he had written, the words sank down deep. They grabbed at his core. No longer were the words of his essay just an intellectual exercise; the words had become much more. They had become words of his heart, words he deeply believed in, words of truth that defined a grave injustice in his world and in his life.

Awakened and changed by these words of truth, Clarkson knew he had to do something. While riding his horse on a country road just outside London, Clarkson dismounted, fell to his knees, and looked up to heaven. That very moment, on his knees, he committed his life and his cause before God to the abolishment of slavery.

With his life's new mission, Clarkson charged forward into action. He translated his prize-winning essay from Latin into English and started distributing it for others to hear. Tens of thousands of copies were printed and distributed throughout England. Those precious words were his instrument to influence and change others just as Clarkson himself had been influenced and changed.

In the face of real dangers and threats, Clarkson never stopped working. He never stopped writing. He never stopped talking about the horrors and the injustice of slavery. Even in his diary, Clarkson would write of his "undaunted spirit" and the determination "that no labour should make me shrink, nor danger, nor even persecution, deter me from my pursuit."

Slowly, progressively, remarkably, men and woman began to listen to Clarkson's words. Day by day, his writings began to open people's minds and, even more importantly, hearts.

Over time, many in Britain joined his cause. They included John Newton, a former slave ship captain and the man who wrote the hymn *Amazing Grace*; Josiah Wedgwood, the famed pottery entrepreneur who commissioned the creation of plates and medallions trumpeting the inhumanity and injustice of slavery; and even members of Parliament such as William Wilberforce.

It took twenty years, but in 1807, Clarkson's words and tireless efforts were rewarded with an approved act of Parliament that forever outlawed the trading of slaves. This victory was followed by legislation passed in 1833 that freed all slaves throughout the British Empire, including its colonies.

Heralded by groups around the globe, these new British laws became a model for the peaceful emancipation of slaves in many distant lands. Even a young America took notice!

With his life's cause fulfilled, Clarkson died peacefully in 1846. He was eighty-six.

The concrete monument erected to memorialize Clarkson's life and work still stands outside London. It was erected on the very spot where Clarkson fell to his knees and dedicated his life to God. It marks the place where a young man's written words became a heart-directed vision, one that forever changed the course of so many lives and so much injustice.

Personal Reflections

Through simple steps—steps such as study, meditation, verbalization, prayer, and willing desire—I can fill my heart with God's priceless Word of wisdom and promise.

By applying my heart to God's Word, I can change my life and inspire the lives of so many other people around me.

PART II

THE VOICE OF FAITH

OUTWARD EXPRESSION

5

Your Voice: Putting Faith into Action

"The water does not flow until the faucet is turned on."
—Louis L' Amour

In Part I, we dug a deep foundation together in the arena we call faith. We now recognize the importance of trusting Father God and the Lord Jesus Christ. We know, too, that we must internalize God's Word as the treasured source for our heart and the blueprint for our life. We also understand the role of our spirit along with the Holy Spirit in this inward process of trusting and believing.

But where do we go from here? A foundation is dug into the ground to be built on. Likewise, a plan or blueprint is created to be acted on. A plan, a blueprint, and a foundation, in and of themselves, carry few if any benefits until we do something with them.

It's no different with faith. Our faith does little good if it sits dormant in a pew or sleeping in a chair. Dormancy won't change our circumstances or revolutionize our life. Dormancy certainly won't give the world around us "a demonstration of the Spirit's power" (1 Cor. 2:4) with its problem-shattering victories.

So what do we do? How do we translate our faith into God's awesome power? How do we take the treasure we have on the inside and use it to achieve life-altering results on the outside? To put it simply: What do we do with our faith once we have it?

Thankfully, the answer is as direct as the questions presented. The primary way we release our trust in God and our belief in his Word is through our mouth and our hands.

Yes, the words we speak from our mouth and the work of our hands are the mediums through which we express what's living in our heart. That's how we unleash God's power into the world around us.

A prominent word to describe this process of expression is "voice." Through our words and deeds, we give a voice to our trust in God and our belief in his promises. This is the voice that God intended each of us to have. This is the voice that our problems and concerns must respond to. This is the voice of faith—our voice of faith.

God instructed Joshua about this important voice when he was training him to become Israel's leader. God told him, "Do not let this book of the law depart from your mouth . . . Then you will be prosperous and successful" (Josh. 1:8).

Substitute the word voice for the word mouth in this Scripture and the meaning will jump out at you: "Do not let this book of the law depart from your voice!"

"Keep speaking, keep expressing, keep voicing your faith in me and in my Word" was what God was teaching him.

For Joshua to be successful, he needed him to understand both the internal heart of faith and the external voice of faith, as the two go hand in hand. If Joshua was to succeed as Israel's leader, he would need to fill both his heart and his mouth with God's Word.

God gave us the same instruction in Proverbs when he told us to store his words in our heart so his truth would be "ready on our lips"—ready to be externalized or voiced into our life. He said, "Apply your heart to what I teach for it is pleasing when you keep them in your heart and have all of them ready on your lips" (Prov. 22:17-18).

Internalize then externalize. Store up, give out. Breathe in, breathe out.

From the inside to the outside, our faith was designed to run and flow. In both words and deeds, our faith was meant to be released in every area of our life.

TURNING ON THE FAUCET

The American writer Louis L'Amour once offered us these words of wisdom: "The water does not flow until the faucet is turned on."

At first glance, L'Amour's words are easy to dismiss. But then, like a knockout punch, the words suddenly hit you. Pow! The wisdom is direct and deep and reveals so much about our life, especially the voice of faith we each need.

Yes, this simple metaphor takes us to the very crux of what we must understand about our voice, which is to get the water of God's power and blessings flowing, we must do something to release it—we must open the faucet, the faucet that is our mouth! It's that basic, that elemental, that essential.

Thinking, analyzing, believing: These inward steps alone, though essential, won't get us the final results we desire for our life. The results and blessings come when we turn on the faucet with our words and other actions.

Are you yearning for the floodgates of heaven's blessings to be opened wide in your life? Do you want to experience God's power flowing more abundantly in all your circumstances? Are there problems and obstacles you desperately need to have moved aside?

Then it's time to get proactive with your faith. It's time to use your voice. It's time to turn on the faucet of God's power and blessings through your faith-filled words and faith-inspired deeds.

In his letter to the early churches, James repeatedly stressed this message of action. He told believers that "faith by itself, if it is not accompanied by action, is dead" (James 2:17). "As the body without the spirit is dead, so faith without deeds is dead" (James 2:26).

To reinforce his point, James reminded believers of Abraham's walk of faith. Abraham took action in response to the trust he had in God. He didn't allow his faith to sit silently in a corner or collect dust on a shelf. He did something with it.

"You see that [Abraham's] faith and his actions were working together, and his faith was made complete by what he did," stressed James (James 2:22).

Only by acting did Abraham complete the spiritual circuit that allowed God's power and blessings to flow fully in his life. Abraham turned on the faucet. He gave voice to his faith. He translated his inward trust out into God's abundant blessings.

The life of Thomas Clarkson is another excellent example. Clarkson didn't sit silently with his beliefs; he opened his mouth. By constantly writing and speaking about the horrors and injustice of slavery, Clarkson acted on what he believed in. He turned the faucet wide open in his life.

Consider the alternative: What if Clarkson had not acted? Would he have accomplished anything for the cause of abolition? Certainly not. Only by giving voice to his heartfelt beliefs did he achieve the end results he so desired.

God has designed our life of faith to be precisely that—a dynamic life filled with vibrant, outward expression. When we open our mouth and give voice to what we trust and believe in our heart, we will always see God's powerful hand moving for our benefit. If, however, we sit dormant in a corner, refusing to act or speak, we will miss out on many of God's blessings for our life, family, and community.

BEING A DOER OF THE WORD

The Bible has another helpful way of bringing out the importance of faith in action: It tells us to be "doers of the word" and "not hearers only."

Look again at the first chapter of James for this instructional message:

> Do not merely listen to the word, and so deceive yourselves. Do what it says. Anyone who listens to the word but does not do what it says is like a man who looks at his face in a mirror and, after looking at himself, goes away and immediately forgets what he looks like.
>
> But the man who looks intently into the perfect law that gives freedom, and continues to do this, not forgetting what he has heard, but doing it—he will be blessed in what he does. (James 1:22-25)

In the gospel of Luke, Jesus taught us the same lesson about being a doer of God's word:

> Why do you call me, "Lord, Lord," and not do what I
> say? I will show you what he is like who comes to me
> and hears my words and puts them into practice. He
> is like a man building a house, who dug down deep
> and laid the foundation on rock. When a flood came,
> the torrent struck that house but could not shake it,
> because it was well built.
>
> But the one who hears my words and does not put
> them into practice is like a man who built a house
> on the ground without a foundation. The moment
> the torrent struck that house, it collapsed and its
> destruction was complete. (Luke 6:46-49)

As members of God's family, we are each called to take the treasure of God's Word and put it into action in our life. Faith leads and inspires us into action if we want to experience the powerful force of change that will revolutionize our life.

The popular poet and writer Ralph Waldo Emerson spoke of this need for action when he wrote, "The greatest homage we can pay to truth is to use it."

Use it, act on it, express it—don't sit on it or put it on a glass shelf. Put God's Word of truth into action in every area of your life. Exercise its precious wisdom in all you say and do. This is the greatest tribute you can pay to God and his wisdom. In return, you will experience God's power and blessings triumphing in your life. God has made you that promise.

MACK TRUCK FAITH

In writing this book, I searched for other ways to help emphasize the message of faith in action. While driving one day, a commercial for an engineering company came on the radio. The announcer described the services this particular engineering firm could provide, and then the announcer quoted a fundamental principle of physics: force equals mass times acceleration.

I know little about engineering and even less about physics, but I immediately knew this principle was helpful to our message.

In a nutshell, the principle says that to create force, you must put an object into motion. Mass or weight alone is not enough. Only when an object is put into motion will a force be created.

For example, if you stood in a parking lot next to a parked Mack truck, the truck would exert no force against you. If, however, someone started the engine and put the massive truck into gear, an overwhelming force would be created, one that would move you and whatever else was in its way.

We need to look at faith in a similar way. Going back to James 2:17, the Scripture tells us that "faith by itself, if it is not accompanied by action, is dead." Just like that parked Mack truck, there's no force—it's dead weight—until we put it into motion.

It's when we put our faith into motion through our words and deeds that we create an overwhelming force—the overwhelming force of God—to crush our problems and benefit our lives.

In his letter to the Philippians, Paul shared this dynamic formula for faith in action. Using his own life as an example, Paul exhorted these early believers to do something with their faith in God. Paul said to them, "Whatever you have learned or received or heard from me, or seen in me—put it into practice. And the God of peace will be with you" (Phil. 4:9).

Paul's life is certainly an ideal example for each of us to follow. In all his words and his deeds, Paul put his faith into motion. He had an unceasing and unwavering voice. In response, God was constantly moving in Paul's life. Everywhere Paul traveled, God's hand moved mightily with miraculous results.

YOUR WORDS ARE ACTIONS

In more than thirty years of ministry, I've traveled to almost every corner of the globe, preaching and teaching God's principles of putting faith into action. Yet no matter where I've traveled—from large urban cities to small rural towns—people share a common misunderstanding about words: Most people don't understand that their words are actions that either advance their life or limit it.

Think about this. For many people, words are little more than waves of sound, tiny bits of rolling amplitude that reverberate in space for a few seconds only to disappear. That's it. Words are a dime a dozen. Inconsequential. Trivial in the grand scheme of life.

In the Bible, however, God gives us an entirely different understanding about words. He tells us that our words are actions—major-league, result-producing, consequence-generating action. The kind of action that puts our faith into motion. The kind of action that drives our goals and advances our dreams. The kind of action that shapes the course of our earthly journey.

God says, "Death and life are in the power of the tongue; and they that love it shall eat the fruit thereof" (Prov. 18:21 KJV).

Look also at the contemporary translation of this verse from Proverbs, which offers up God's wisdom about our words in these striking terms: "Words kill, words give life; they're either poison or fruit—you choose" (Prov. 18:21 MSG).

Jesus gave us the same thought-provoking, life-challenging message about the consequences of our words. He told us that our words will create either constructive or destructive consequences in our life:

> Let me tell you something: Every one of these careless words is going to come back to haunt you. There will be a time of reckoning. Words are powerful; take them seriously. Words can be your salvation. Words can also be your damnation. (Matt. 12:36-37 MSG)

There will be a time of reckoning for everyone. Our words don't just randomly bounce around for a brief moment only to disappear. The words we speak are lasting and powerful actions that impact and affect everything and everyone around us. They are producers and influencers, even to the point of life and death. We must take them seriously. We must handle them wisely.

Examine your life: If you're not succeeding, if you're not achieving your goals, look at what you're routinely saying. If you're losing ground or struggling in certain areas, look closely at the words you're continually releasing. If you want more of something or less of something in your life, change your words.

Change your words, and you change your relationships. Change your words, and you change the entire dynamic around you. It's true. God told us it's true.

Your Words Produce a Harvest

Whenever I think about words as actions, the 1984 "Bless You Boys" Detroit Tigers season always comes to mind. That season left an indelible mark on me and encouraged me to dig deeply into God's wisdom about our speaking. Even today, I still marvel about that special time in Detroit and how an entire city instinctively grabbed onto words—words of support and encouragement—recognizing that those words, once spoken, would produce results.

"Bless you boys! Bless you boys!": I can hear the echoes. The words filled the streets; the words consumed every voice. People wouldn't stop saying it; people couldn't stop saying it. It was contagious. It was refreshing.

Sure, part of it was simply "good fun" and the exuberance of fans—but only a part. The other part—the undeniable part—was that the people of Detroit genuinely took hold of these words. They purposed to say them. They took them seriously. During that season, their words became their determined actions—actions that had a great impact.

In his book *Wire to Wire,* sportswriter George Cantor pointed out how these words—"Bless you boys!"—were much more than a funny bit or an ironic slogan. "It became a description of how Detroit fans, from little old ladies to hairy-knuckled workers on the Ford line, really felt about this team," wrote Cantor. The words were sincere and purposeful—and they produced results.

In the end, what the people of Detroit experienced through their words was a harvest for their team, their community, and themselves. Through their words, they created the rewards that God specifically told us about when he said, "From the fruit of his lips a man is filled with good things as surely as the work of his hands rewards him" (Prov. 12:14).

God also highlighted this principle in Prov. 18:20 when he declared, "From the fruit of his mouth a man's stomach is filled; with the harvest from his lips he is satisfied."

Just as our hands produce for us in life so do our words. Words grow fruit. Words create a harvest of rewards—the "good things" we desire for our life. Our words, like our deeds, are actions that build, craft, and create what we will enjoy in life.

I like how Paul put the proposition when he called our words a form of "doing." He said, "Whatever you do, whether in word or deed, do it all in the name of the Lord Jesus, giving thanks to God the Father through him" (Col. 3:17).

Paul understood the significance of our words, and he wanted us to appreciate and esteem every word we send forth. He knew that our words would either advance the goals of God and Christ on the earth or limit them.

YOUR WORDS WIELD GOD'S HAMMER

In the book of Jeremiah, God provides another fundamental lesson about our words as actions. He tells us our faith-filled words set in motion his unrelenting spiritual power.

Look at how God dramatically describes this supernatural force created by our words of faith:

> "Let the one who has my word speak it faithfully. For what has straw to do with grain?" declares the Lord. "Is not my word like fire," declares the Lord, "and like a hammer that breaks a rock in pieces?" (Jer. 23:28-29)

God's Word spoken in faith over our life is the spiritual hammer that pulverizes our problems and the raging fire that consumes the unhelpful, unwanted, and unnecessary obstacles in our path. No adversary can withstand its pounding; no circumstance can put out its scorching flames. Against every enemy, the spoken word of faith is unstoppable.

In his letters to the early churches, Paul confirmed God's message in Jeremiah by likening our words of faith to a divine sword—"the sword of the Spirit."

"Take the helmet of salvation and the sword of the Spirit, which is the word of God," Paul wrote in Eph. 6:17. Paul wanted believers to employ and engage this supernatural weapon in all life's battles and conquests.

In Mark's gospel, Jesus also spoke about this unstoppable spiritual weapon given to believers. He even gave a firsthand demonstration of its power when he cursed a fig tree, causing the tree to shrivel from its roots upward.

When the disciples who were with Jesus witnessed what had happened to that tree, they were astonished and pressed Jesus for answers.

In response, Jesus explained that what they had heard and seen was simply faith in action—faith in God taken from the heart and released through words. He told them, "I tell you the truth, if anyone says to this mountain, 'Go throw yourself into the sea,' and does not doubt in his heart but believes that what he says will happen, it will be done for him" (Mark 11:22-23).

The Physicality of Speech

What else can we learn about our words as actions? Let's ask another knowledgeable group: language experts. After all, these experts, called linguists, spend their lives studying how we speak. They research and examine the intricacies of our language, from the letters and punctuation marks we use to the ancient roots of our modern-day tongues.

Not surprisingly, linguists agree on some things but disagree on much more. Like experts in every academic field, they each have their own views and differing theories. What's enlightening, however, is that linguists do agree on two universal points.

First, they agree that words are mankind's unique and distinctive gift, a gift shared by no other creature on planet earth. Second, these experts agree that the spoken word—what we call speech—involves the extraordinary physical action of the human body.

It's fascinating. They have found that to utter even a single spoken word, the human body must engage hundreds of different muscle groups and a full array of body systems, including our lungs, throat, tongue, teeth, lips, and nose. The human body must be fully engaged for us to speak.

X-ray studies on speech production have also confirmed this intricate, complex, and sweeping involvement of the human body. On an X-ray, hundreds of different muscles can be seen twisting and turning as we speak. And just as remarkably, these muscles must act and engage with near-perfect precision for even a single spoken word to come forth.

To speak is an extraordinary physical achievement. To speak is physical action at its finest.

Your Actions Are Words

When we realize that our words are actions, our focus rightly changes. We begin to consider our words. We begin to guide our words. We begin to have a purpose for what we say and how we say it.

With this new focus, however, there comes potential risks: the risks of using our words as a compromise for our personal conduct and a justification for not helping others. Let's face it: Sometimes it's a lot easier to say something rather than change one's behavior or jump in with a helping hand.

But we know that words alone won't cut it. Our Christian voice is made up of words and deeds. It's this balance that keeps us on the correct path and away from deceptive extremes. Indeed, God's message in the Bible repeatedly stresses that our words, no matter how faith-filled and commendable, will never mask sinful conduct or faithless behavior.

God instructs each of us to live right and love others. He asks us to work with integrity. He asks us to forgive others. He asks us to give, help, and serve people within our families, workplaces, and communities. "This is my command," said Jesus, "Love each other" (John 15:17).

"Whoever loves his brother lives in the light, and there is nothing in him to make him stumble" (1 John 2:10).

From this message also comes the realization that our conduct, behavior, and service—our love for others—is what "speaks" so profoundly to everyone around us. Our conduct and our service are the clearest and most persuasive "words" we will ever have for communicating our faith to others. It's the age-old wisdom of actions speaking louder than words.

I enjoy what Andrew Carnegie, the legendary U.S. financier, often said in this regard: "As I grow older, I pay less attention to what people say. I just watch what they do."

In his letter to believers, James made the same point about the persuasive message our actions communicate to others. He stressed the need for believers to express their faith not just in words but through works of service and charity. It's not enough to show your faith only in words, said James, but we must "show [our] faith by what [we] do" (James 2:18).

I also enjoy what Gen. Colin Powell, the great military leader and adviser, said about the frank and candid message our conduct expresses to others. Talking about the love of his parents and the lessons they taught him growing up, he said, "The greatest gifts my parents gave me . . . were their unconditional love and a set of values—values that they lived and didn't just lecture about."

Christian values lived out daily are the greatest gifts and the greatest message we can give to the people around us. These living values constitute the most inspiring "words" we will ever express to those in need of Jesus Christ. They are truly the underlying message of the gospel and the overriding message of our Father's kingdom.

As you and I journey together through the pages of this book, let's keep our perspective by always remembering that our words are actions and our actions are words. Both are essential for a successful and faith-filled life.

Your Attitude Broadcasts Your Beliefs

To complete this discussion, there's one last point that needs to be made—something we usually overlook about our voice in life: Our daily attitude broadcasts our beliefs! Each day, our attitude expresses what we believe and whom we trust.

Look around you: What does the attitude of your spouse, boss, or coworkers tell you about them, their day, and their life? What do their attitudes express about the things they value and the people they trust?

How about you? What did your attitude broadcast about you today? What did it reveal about your outlook on life? What did it signal about the beliefs you hold and the placement of your trust?

These are probing questions, aren't they? They force us to closely examine our life and our faith.

These questions also point us back to the lesson of the early Israelites and how their attitude revealed a lack of trust in God. Remember how they constantly grumbled and complained as they traveled from Egypt to the Promised Land. "They grumbled in their tents" because "they did not believe [God's] promise" is how the Bible describes this (Ps. 106:24-25).

The Israelites' daily attitude acknowledged their distrust of the Lord and their disbelief in his promises.

In a sad and angry response, God said to Moses, "How long will these people treat me with contempt? How long will they refuse to believe in me?" (Num. 14:11).

If we trust God, we can't constantly grumble and complain about our lives. If we believe God's promises, we can't continually be negative, crabby, and irritable in our homes, schools, and workplaces. If we're constantly "grumbling in our tents," then we don't believe God or his promises. A heart filled with faith and a habitually negative attitude simply can't coexist.

When we trust God for help, support, and change, our attitude will be a reflection of that inward trust. A positive attitude, one filled with encouragement and expectation, evidences a heart that believes God is in charge of our circumstances and is working to bring about the blessings and changes we desire, all in his perfect timing.

When God told us in Prov. 3:5-6 to trust him with all our heart and "in all [our] ways, acknowledge him," his guidance most definitely included our attitude.

Through this daily approach to life, God looks for us to express our trust in him. Through our daily attitude, he asks us to acknowledge all his promises. In return, God has promised to make our paths straight, true, and abundantly blessed.

Personal Reflections

Through my words, deeds, and attitude, I give a voice to my faith and move God's mighty hand into my life and all my circumstances.

My words are actions, actions that produce definite results, certain consequences, and lasting rewards.

With a heart filled with faith and a wide-open mouth, I turn on the faucet of God's blessings for my life, family, and community.

6

Steering Your Course

"I am very little inclined on any occasion to say anything unless I hope to produce some good by it."
—*Abraham Lincoln*

"It's time to use our words to declare good things!"
—*Joel Osteen*

The more we learn about the powerful force and creative impact of our words, the better able and more determined we become about harnessing our words so they work for us, not against us. With words on our side, we can steer our life's journey in positive directions that allow us to reach our goals and accomplish our dreams.

In this chapter, let's explore more of God's wisdom about our speaking. By examining God's wisdom, I want to change your perspective forever about the words you speak.

RUDDERS, PADDLES, AND TINY BITS

One of the most thought-provoking comparisons on the role of our words comes from the book of James. It's here that our tongue is compared with the rudder of a ship or the small metal bit we place in a horse's mouth. Though both the rudder and the bit are extremely small, these are the instruments we use to direct the course of massive ships and control the movement of mighty horses.

Our tongue plays a similar role: It's the small but dynamic instrument we use to control and direct our course in life. With our tongue, we can steer past problems and head out for crystal-blue open waters. With our tongue, we can set our course for exotic islands and safe harbors. Yet with that same tongue, we can head straight for the jagged rocks and utter disaster.

With our tongues, we can accomplish anything or destroy everything:

> A bit in the mouth of a horse controls the whole horse. A small rudder on a huge ship in the hands of a skilled captain sets a course in the face of the strongest winds. A word out of your mouth may seem of no account, but it can accomplish nearly anything—or destroy it! (James 3:3-5 MSG)

Over the years, I've searched for other examples to highlight the life-directing role of our tongue. One comparison that has always helped guide me is a boat with two paddles.

In your mind, picture a sturdy wooden boat with two paddles. One paddle represents your words; the other paddle represents your personal conduct. These are the two paddles you must use to steer your course and propel your journey.

But what happens if your paddles are pulling in opposite directions? What's the end result? What happens to your boat?

The end result is this: Your boat ends up spinning in circles, going nowhere except where the currents and the problems of life decide to take it!

Take a look around you. How many spinning and drifting boats do you see out there? Far too many, right? A few of these boats may get lucky and hit shore without great damage. Most, however, will sink, crash, or get lost at sea. Just turn on the news to hear the constant stream of catastrophic stories.

And what about Christians? How many Christian boats do you see spinning and drifting out there? No one's immune. No one's exempt. Even as Christians, our words will rob us of success in life if we don't harness and direct them. God explained this difficult truth to us in the Bible by saying, "If anyone considers himself religious and yet does not keep a tight rein on his tongue, he deceives himself and his religion is worthless" (James 1:26).

That's sobering, isn't it? Our words can and will rob us if we don't weigh, consider, and control them. It doesn't matter how much we try to puff ourselves up by focusing on our church attendance, prayer life, and other religious and spiritual endeavors—if we fail to harness our tongue, we forfeit so much.

Look also at what God tells us in the book of Proverbs about the consequences created by our tongue. Here God explicitly cautions us in three jarring verses:

- "A fool's mouth is his undoing, and his lips are a snare to his soul." (Prov. 18:7)

- "Do you see a man who speaks in haste? There is more hope for a fool than for him." (Prov. 29:20)

- "He who guards his mouth and his tongue keeps himself from calamity." (Prov. 21:23)

No one wants to be foolish. No one wants to be snared, undone, or left without hope. No one wants to fall into calamity. But these are the real consequences of untethered, unbridled, and uncontrolled words. It's up to us to take control of our tongue so our words work for us, not against us.

If we learn to control and direct our words, we will benefit in every area of life. The Bible goes so far as to tell us that if we gain control over our words, we will reach a place where we gain mastery over our entire body: "We all stumble in many ways. [But] if anyone is never at fault in what [he or she] says, [that person] is a perfect [person], able to keep [his or her] whole body in check" (James 3:2).

Is there a bad habit or behavior you're struggling with or want to eliminate? Are there aspects of your life that you want to master? Begin by focusing on your words. Start to control what you say both to yourself and others. Think about your words before you let them escape your lips. Grab hold of your words; harness them to pull you in the direction you want to go.

Through small steps, day after day, you can learn to control, guide, and direct your words. Over time, this mastery will grow, and it will translate into mastery in many other areas of your life. The rewards are great.

INCENDIARY SPARKS

Havoc, chaos, dark smoke, and blazing fires—we've seen "infernos" throughout history—all started by words. It takes only a handful of incendiary sparks—fiery little words—to ignite a blaze that causes overwhelming destruction. The Bible describes the scene and the escalating consequences:

> It only takes a spark, remember, to set off a forest
> fire. A careless or wrongly placed word out of your
> mouth can do that.
>
> By our speech, we can ruin the world, turn harmony
> to chaos, throw mud on a reputation, send the whole
> world up in smoke and go up in smoke with it, smoke
> right from the pit of hell. (James 3:6 MSG)

The book of Proverbs further details the destructive consequences
our words can cause by declaring, "With his mouth the godless
destroys his neighbor" (Prov. 11:9).

The book of Psalms completes the picture by comparing the
destructive words of men and women to swords and deadly arrows.
"Hide me from the conspiracy of the wicked, from that noisy crowd
of evildoers. They sharpen their tongues like swords and aim their
words like deadly arrows" (Ps. 64:2-3).

Forest fires, incendiary sparks, sharpened swords, and deadly
arrows: These images from the Bible are harsh but candid. They
reveal the deep wounds and deadly destruction our words can cause
in the world and lives of others. Whenever I reflect on these images, I
can't help but look back at the words I've spoken to others. What did
I say? How did I say it? Could I have said something more helpful,
more mindful of others?

I think about the description poet Pearl Strachen Hurd gave me about
my words: "Handle them carefully, for words have more power than
atom bombs!" What bombs did I drop? What damage did I cause?
More importantly, I ask myself: How do I avoid these words in the
future so I can continue to improve?

Of course, it's not just my intentional words that cause harm; my
"careless or wrongly placed words" can do damage as well. We've all
experienced situations and relationships where careless or misplaced

words have caused turmoil, strife, and hurt feelings. Even a small handful of misplaced words are sometimes enough to jeopardize events and endanger relationships.

And don't forget the other category of "careless or wrongly placed words" we all know too well: gossip. Yes, gossip has damaging effects and harmful consequences. God's wisdom tells us that gossip fuels the fire of human discord. It harms friendships, burns bridges, and escalates conflict.

Prov. 26:20 puts it like this: "Without wood a fire goes out; without gossip a quarrel dies down." By refusing to engage in gossip, we remove the fuel that perpetuates so much conflict. By refusing to gossip, we promote love and strengthen our relationships. "[Whoever] covers over an offense promotes love, but whoever repeats the matter separates close friends" (Prov. 17:9).

I know gossip is not easy to avoid. Marketed twenty-four seven, bits of gossip are constantly whispered for us to hear and respond to. Plus, these words can seem like "choice morsels"—they go down easy. Am I right?

But gossip, in the end, nourishes no one; it serves only to pollute the air and all those who listen. I like the way Proverbs explains the matter for us in language even a child would appreciate: "Listening to gossip is like eating cheap candy; do you really want junk like that in your belly?" (Prov. 18:8 MSG).

Be careful with gossip. Avoid it. That's God's wisdom for us. The Bible even counsels us to be careful around people who habitually gossip. "Gossips can't keep secrets," we are told, "so never confide in blabbermouths" (Prov. 20:19 MSG). "A gadabout gossip can't be trusted with a secret, but someone of integrity won't violate a confidence" (Prov. 11:13 MSG). Good advice.

GOLDEN APPLES

In this chapter, I've focused much attention on the destructive side of words, but there's a constructive side that's even more important to emphasize. If God makes anything unmistakably clear to us in the Bible, it's that our words can be the greatest source of lasting good for the lives of those they touch.

"Reckless words pierce like a sword, but the tongue of the wise brings healing," we are told (Prov. 12:18).

With the power of our words, you and I can bring help, healing, and support to countless people in the world around us. Our words can change lives, circumstances, and events—all for the good. "The mouth of the righteous is a fountain of life" (Prov. 10:11). "The lips of the righteous nourish many" (Prov. 10:21). What a remarkable gift we each can share.

Also consider this: Whenever evil words are sent out, potentially bringing harm to others, our godly words are able to rescue people. "The words of the wicked lie in wait for blood, but the speech of the upright rescues them" (Prov. 12:6).

Through words of faith, love, and encouragement, we can reach out to rescue those who are suffering and those who are in need. Think about all the lives we can lift and support today just by reaching out with our beneficial words. Young and old, rich or poor—everyone has a need.

One of the other highlights of God's wisdom on the beneficial qualities of our words comes from Prov. 25:11. Here God shares with us this most valuable truth: "A word aptly spoken is like apples of gold in settings of silver."

What a vivid and rewarding image of the lasting value our words can have in the lives of those they touch. Through the words we speak, we can give out "golden apples in settings of silver" to our family, friends, colleagues, and all those we encounter in life. Real value. Real assistance. Real meaning. All through words—our words.

It's not difficult. Even one word can have this value in someone's life. I like how Mother Teresa often emphasized this point by describing the "endless echoes" of speaking a simple, kind word. She said, "Kind words can be short and easy to speak, but their echoes are endless."

NEVER REPAY EVIL WITH EVIL

We know our words can open the faucet of God's blessings, but they can close that faucet tight as well. Through evil words—words of harm, insult, and deceit—we can close the storehouse of heaven and cause famine in our lives.

God makes this strong point to us in the Bible by saying, "Whoever of you loves life and desires to see many good days, keep your tongue from evil and your lips from speaking lies. Turn from evil and do good; seek peace and pursue it" (Ps. 34:12-14).

In his letter to believers, Peter stressed this same important truth. To enjoy a long and blessed life, he told believers to avoid evil words just as they would evil deeds. Avoid evil, hurtful, harmful words, he said, even when others insult you, curse you, or speak wrongly against you. Never repay evil with evil or insult with insult. Do just the opposite—offer words of blessings and kindness in return:

> Do not repay evil with evil or insult with insult, but
> with blessing, because to this you were called so that
> you may inherit a blessing. (1 Peter 3:9)

Peter shared how God always listens and continually moves in the lives of those who promote peace and goodwill. Drawing from the words of Psalm 34, Peter wrote:

> Whoever wants to embrace life and see the day filled up with good, here's what you do: Say nothing evil or hurtful; snub evil and cultivate good; run after peace for all you're worth.

> God looks on all this with approval, listening and responding well to what he's asked; but he turns his back on those who do evil things. (1 Peter 3:10-12 MSG)

God's wisdom for us is clear: "The one who blesses others is abundantly blessed; those who help others are helped" (Prov. 11:25 MSG). And the flip side: "He loved to pronounce a curse—may it come on him; he found no pleasure in blessing—may it be far from him" (Ps. 109:17).

If you want abundant blessings, bless others. If you want help, help others. If you want support and encouragement in your own life, then give that out to those around you. Use your words and deeds as the catalyst for bringing blessings and good things into your life and into the lives of the people who surround you.

WHAT WILL YOUR ACCOUNT BE?

God created us in his own image and likeness, and that extraordinary resemblance definitely includes the gift of words. The gift of words is our God-given instrument for creating the life we want to live.

With this gift, we can accomplish anything. We can shape today's events and influence tomorrow's responses. We can change human behavior and alter human emotions. Laughter, excitement, anger, disappointment, and sorrow: These emotions can be triggered by a mere handful of words. From the oratory of a politician to the jokes of a comedian or the gentle encouragement of a friend, words craft, create, and give life to our human world.

With the gift of words, we can inspire success and foster achievement. With words, we can give our minds the opportunity to share the rich and complex ideas that, in turn, inspire others to think, dream, and create. Words are a wondrous gift that orchestrates, perpetuates, and enables all these adventures and mankind's most amazing accomplishments.

On the spiritual level, our faith-filled words release God's power for change and position us to receive so many of his blessings. The voice of faith swings God's mighty hammer and ignites his all-consuming fire. And our words spoken to God in prayer impact this planet and every element of our lives.

The gift of words plays a starring role in life on every level. When we get to heaven, God will ask what we did with this gift. We will give an account to him of all the words we have spoken. "But I tell you that [people] will have to give account on the day of judgment for every careless word they have spoken," explained Jesus (Matt. 12:36).

So what will we say? What will our account be?

Will we explain how we used our words like golden apples to enrich lives? Or will we regret the incendiary sparks and deadly arrows we sent forth that caused so much harm? Will we tell God that we blessed and encouraged others or that we used our words to curse men and women and to spread hatred and ignorance?

Will we rejoice at the long and lasting legacy of help and support our words created in the lives they touched? Or will we deeply regret the trail of sorrow and hurt they inflicted?

These questions will be asked—and answered. Thankfully, the answers are up to us.

If you've used your words poorly in the past, purpose to change starting today. Begin to speak beneficial words, helpful words, healing words. Begin to speak words of support and encouragement in your own life and in the lives of others. Take the opportunity each day to give golden apples to your children, spouse, coworkers, and friends. Lift someone's day with a kind word and a gentle smile.

Guide your words and let them take you into new realms and higher heights. Make your words work for you, not against you. Make your words a blessing for all they touch and everyone they encounter.

YOUR ONE-THING EXERCISE

Before we conclude this chapter, let me challenge you with an exercise. For one week, start each day by asking yourself this simple question: What one thing can I say today to benefit the people in my life? That's your question. Don't look for two things or three things—just one thing. What one thing can I say today?

For my spouse, what one thing can I say to encourage him or her today? For my children, what one thing can I say to inspire and build self-confidence in them? For my coworkers, what one thing can I say to help them and advance our workplace? You will amaze yourself at what pops into your mind when you ask yourself this question.

But don't stop there: Go out and speak the words! Give out your golden apples! If you will speak the words, you will astound yourself by their impact on others. It will change their lives and your life.

Personal Reflections

My words are my gift and my instrument for guiding, propelling, and creating the life I want to live. With words as my rudder and paddle, I can steer my journey in the direction of my goals and dreams.

My words can be golden apples in settings of silver that enrich lives—or incendiary sparks that destroy lives. The decision is mine.

With my words, I can open the faucet of God's divine blessings or I can close that faucet tight.

7

Faith-Filled Words:
"I Believe, Therefore I Speak"

"So when you take words from the Bible and put them in your heart and in your mouth, they bring what they promise—supernatural things!"

—Gloria Copeland

In this chapter, I want to drill deeper and examine more closely the subject of faith-filled words. The greater our understanding of these special words, the better equipped we will be for life's challenges, problems, and concerns—and the more certain our victories will be.

Of all the words we will ever speak, these are the words of the heart that must take center stage in our life.

THE EXPRESSION OF THE HEART

All great artists and performers, regardless of their medium—be it music, dance, painting, sculpture—ultimately come to one realization: Truly meaningful, life-changing expression comes from the heart. From deep inside, from our innermost well, comes the inspiration, creativity, and desire that distinguishes the magnificent from the common, the exceptional from the standard, the genuine from the imitation.

Legendary ballet dancer Mikhail Baryshnikov embraced this realization throughout his career on stage. He said, "There comes a moment in a young artist's life when he knows he has to bring something to the stage from within himself."

This inward-driven expression, stressed Baryshnikov, was what distinguished every dancer and elevated every performance. Without it, the extraordinary would never be created on stage, on canvas, in song—or in life.

Centuries earlier, Leonardo da Vinci brought out this same message when he wrote, "Where the spirit does not work with the hand, there is no art."

Art—true art—is a work of both the heart and the hand. The hand alone, no matter how trained and skilled, will never create a Mona Lisa. The hand alone, no matter how well schooled and practiced, will never paint a Monet landscape, a Rembrandt portrait, or a Renoir impression. A person need only gaze for an instant at Michelangelo's *Statue of David* to recognize that this utterly astounding expression came from the artist's heart and not merely the human hand.

Even the great Pablo Picasso was quick to admit that his artistic expression was driven by the artist from within. "Painting is a *jeu d'espirit* [a play of the spirit]," said Picasso of his work.

These same comments apply equally to the world of music. Through the limitless dynamic of music and song, the human spirit has been given an infinite platform for outward expression. The renowned American composer Aaron Copland put it like this: "So long as the human spirit thrives on this planet, music in some living form will accompany and sustain it and give it expressive meaning."

We see this same appreciation reflected in the work of today's most commercial and highly acclaimed singers and songwriters. They, too, understand that the medium we call music only comes to life through an expression of the heart by the artist from within.

A favorite example here is Jennifer Lopez, the magnanimous "J-Lo" to her fans. As part of her first appearance on the hit TV show *American Idol*, Lopez worked with the young and aspiring contestants, mentoring them with her advice for success. Her wisdom for these blossoming young singers was both simple and direct: "Sing from the heart!" You want to connect with your audience, have an impact, and distinguish yourself from the crowd: "Sing from the heart!" That's the key.

Her comments echo those of the ever-talented Stevie Wonder, who has called music "the spirit of song." Through the notes, melodies, and lyrics, men and women can voice who they are on the inside, offering the world a magical look at mankind's most glorious and eternal dimension. For Wonder and all accomplished artists, this is the X-factor—the distinguishing factor—for all life-touching music.

The world of sports is no different. The X-factor is at work in the achievement of every great athlete. "The heart of a champion" is on the inside, expressed through the highly trained muscles and coordinated actions of the body and the mind. Coaches sometimes call this inward-driven achievement a will to win, desire, or passion. Many simply call it heart!

This same idea even applies in the highly competitive business world. In the long run, what distinguishes one company from another isn't the technology, corporate offices, or other external factors often mentioned in corporate brochures. In the long run, what distinguishes a great company from the average company is always the people—the employees.

And it's here, within the hearts of its employees, that the great companies reach the highest levels of achievement and customer service. Hal Rosenbluth, an author and highly regarded business consultant, perhaps said it best when he wrote, "The highest achievable level of service comes from the heart, so the company that reaches its people's hearts will provide the very best service."

FAITH'S SUPERNATURAL UTTERANCE

The above examples highlight the vitality of the inner man and inner woman and the moving voice we each can have in life. But this guidance doesn't stop here. These examples lead us further, pointing us to what God and Jesus are looking for in our faith life as well.

The Christian life of faith is a life of the heart. From out of our innermost self, we are each called to express our faith. Remember what Jesus said: "The kingdom of God is within you" (Luke 17:21)— and that's what we must bring out into our lives and the lives around us.

We can see this life of the heart in the tools God has given us. He's given us a re-created spirit—the heart of a champion—one that is inhabited by the Holy Spirit.

He's given us the infinite and eternal power of his Word. His divine sword and unrelenting hammer.

He's also given us the gift of speech as our instrument for expressing it all. We've been given the extraordinary capability to speak and achieve heaven's greatest goals on the earth.

It's staggering really. By taking what we have on the inside—God's Word treasured in our heart—and releasing this truth through words, we can alter every aspect of our life. With our heart and mouth, we can prompt the hand of God and position his power in the midst of our circumstances.

I love how Gloria Copeland, the devoted minister and beloved woman of God, once described this ability God has given us. She said, "So when you take words from the Bible and put them in your heart and in your mouth, they bring what they promise—supernatural things!"

"I Believe, Therefore I Speak"

Throughout this book, I've described this supernatural process of expression in a variety of ways, including the voice of faith, the sword of the spirit, turning on the faucet, and putting faith into action. Each of these examples has provided a valuable perspective into what we've been given from God.

To complete our understanding, let's look at one last example. It comes from Paul and his letter to the Corinthian church. In his letter, Paul described the heart of faith—or "the spirit of faith" as he called it—that must drive our spiritual voice:

> It is written: "I believed; therefore I have spoken." With that same spirit of faith we also believe and therefore speak, because we know that the one who raised the Lord Jesus from the dead will also raise us with Jesus and present us with you in his presence. (2 Cor. 4:13-14)

In just two sentences, Paul summed up the great results of his ministry. The results came from Paul believing God's Word in his heart and then expressing that with his mouth. It was his heart and his mouth working together. This coordinated action moved God's hand in miraculous ways.

"I believed, therefore I have spoken," said Paul—the voice of faith, which announces and carries God's miracles.

Paul's voice of faith was what God was looking for during the days of the early church. This was the utterance God needed to follow through with signs, miracles, and every form of divine manifestation and deliverance. This was the voice that partnered with God Almighty and the Lord Jesus Christ to change our world forever.

This was the same spiritual voice Abraham and the prophets understood and expressed to accomplish God's miraculous feats. It was also the voice of faith that Jesus understood and expressed throughout his earthly ministry.

Believing God's word in your heart and then releasing that faith from your mouth constitutes the two basic elements of our quintessential principle of spiritual expression. It's the "I believe, therefore I speak" model of faith in action.

If you look closely, you will see this spiritual footprint revealed in many Scriptures in the Bible. Look, for example, at the now-familiar Jeremiah 23:28-29:

> "Let the one who has my word speak it faithfully. For
> what has straw to do with grain?" declares the Lord.
> "Is not my word like fire," declares the Lord, "and
> like a hammer that breaks a rock in pieces?"

Can you see the model here? We, of course, see God's instruction that his word be spoken. But who should do the speaking?

"Let the one who has my word" do the speaking, declares the Lord. Let the Christians who have stored and treasured God's word in their heart be the ones to speak. "I believe, therefore I speak" God's word—and this utterance of the heart becomes the fire that consumes and the hammer that crushes.

Like everything in a life of faith, our trust in God and our belief in his promises establish the necessary foundation. That's why we spent the opening chapters of this book examining the heart of faith and learning how to internalize God's promises. When we've taken the time to store these special words in our heart, we then have treasure to speak into our life.

When we've completed the preparations, God's Word will be the first thing that leaves our mouth to confront our problems and address our concerns. This is the way of wisdom, says the Bible: "The heart of the wise teacheth [the] mouth" (Prov. 16:23 KJV).

YOUR SPIRITUAL VOICE—JESUS EXPLAINS

In the gospels, Jesus had much to say about spiritual expression. One of his important teachings is outlined in chapter 15 of Matthew's gospel.

It's here that Jesus was confronted by a group of Pharisees who questioned why Jesus' disciples had not washed their hands before eating. Under Jewish law, people were required to wash their hands before each meal. Beyond the issue of sanitation, clean hands were supposed to represent a sign of cleanliness before God.

Responding to the open criticism of the Pharisees, Jesus addressed his response to the large crowd that had gathered to hear him teach. He said, "Listen and understand. What goes into a man's mouth does not make him 'unclean,' but what comes out of his mouth that is what makes him 'unclean'" (Matt. 15:10-11).

After the Pharisees huffed off and the crowd dispersed, Peter and the other disciples asked Jesus to explain the meaning of his statement. Jesus explained it like this:

> Don't you see that whatever enters the mouth goes
> into the stomach and then out of the body? But the
> things that come out of the mouth come from the
> heart, and these make a man "unclean."
>
> For out of the heart come evil thoughts, murder,
> adultery, sexual immorality, theft, false testimony,
> slander. These are what make a man "unclean"; but
> eating with unwashed hands does not make him
> "unclean." (Matt. 15:17-20)

Using the term "mouth" instead of our more-familiar term "voice,"
Jesus was describing how men and women express what's in their
heart through their words, deeds, and attitudes. Look at a person's
outward voice or expression—"what comes out of their mouth"—
Jesus told them, for that's how you recognize a person's spiritual
condition. Out of the heart comes the words, deeds, and desires that
reveal whether someone is clean or unclean.

In chapter 6 of Luke's gospel, Jesus provided additional instruction
about mankind's spiritual expression. Addressing a large group of
his disciples, Jesus told them:

> No good tree bears bad fruit, nor does a bad tree bear
> good fruit. Each tree is recognized by its own fruit.
> People do not pick figs from thorn bushes, or grapes
> from briers.
>
> The good man brings good things out of the good stored
> up in his heart, and the evil man brings evil things out
> of the evil stored up in his heart. For out of the overflow
> of his heart his mouth speaks. (Luke 6:43-45)

Again, Jesus talks about the outward expression of our heart—"the
fruit" that is born on the outside in the form of our words, deeds, and
attitude. This fruit, says Jesus, reveals a person's inner condition.

Good trees produce good fruit, just as the good person brings out the good things he or she has stored in his or her heart. The bad tree and the evil person bring out just the opposite.

The King James Version of the Bible uses the word "treasure" in place of the word "things." That's a helpful way of describing it: The good person brings out the "good treasure" he or she has stored in his or her heart, whereas the evil person brings out the "evil treasure."

Only by examining the type of fruit or treasure a person produces can we understand what's going on spiritually. Our eyes can't see or even get a glimpse of the heart; however, we can get a detailed high-resolution image of it by looking at a person's words, deeds, and attitude.

It's what Thomas Edison meant when he said, "What you are will show in what you do." On the outside—in all our doings—we show who we are on the inside. Our outward fruit tells a comprehensive story about us.

FROM THAT WHICH FILLS YOUR HEART

In the last sentence of Luke 6:45, Jesus adds one final point of guidance for us: "For out of the overflow of his heart, his mouth speaks."

The Amplified Bible translates this verse as "For out of the abundance (overflow) of the heart, his mouth speaks." I especially like the New American Standard Bible translation, which puts it like this: "For his mouth speaks from that which fills his heart."

What is Jesus telling us here? What is he explaining about our spiritual voice?

Jesus is telling us that our spiritual "mouth"—the outward, "voiced" words and deeds of our heart—is supplied, fueled, and driven by what we have stored inside. Our spiritual mouth voices—or speaks—"from that which fills [our] heart."

Doesn't this make sense? We can't bring out what we don't have stored on the inside. Unlike our natural mouth, which can fake all kinds of expression, our spiritual mouth is different. You can't fake true spiritual expression; it either comes from the heart or it doesn't. Either you believe it and value it on the inside or you don't.

Jesus emphasized this point to the Pharisees whenever they confronted him with Jewish rules and regulations. Quoting from the book of Isaiah, Jesus would admonish their false and contrived expression before God, saying: "These people honor me with their lips, but their hearts are far from me. They worship me in vain; their teachings are but rules taught by men" (Matt. 15:8-9).

Jesus stressed that the Pharisees were merely giving lip service to God. They were expressing only what they thought was expected of them based on external rules and written guidelines. They weren't expressing what was in their heart—what they truly believed and desired to say before God. Their natural mouths were moving, but their spiritual mouths were not.

These teachings from Jesus remind me of what Hall of Fame musician and saxophonist Charlie Parker once emphasized about musical expression. Speaking to musicians who wanted to imitate his powerful style, Parker said, "If you don't believe it, it won't come out of your horn."

It's no different when it comes to expressing our faith. If we don't genuinely believe something in our heart, it won't come out of our spiritual mouth, our "horn." It won't be genuine; it won't be faith filled. Instead it will be artificial, contrived, and powerless.

And isn't that what God explained to Joshua when he was training Joshua to become Israel's leader?

God taught him to keep studying, meditating, and reflecting on the Book of the Law (God's Word) so this truth would fill and overflow from his heart. By doing so, Joshua's spiritual mouth—his horn—would have God's wisdom and promises ready to be expressed in all the events, problems, and circumstances of his life. Therefore, Joshua's prosperity and success would be ensured.

Look also at Psalm 37 where God, through the words of David, has the same message: "The mouth of the righteous man utters wisdom, and his tongue speaks what is just. The law of his God is in his heart; his feet do not slip" (Ps. 37:30-31).

Because the righteous person sows God's Word in his or her heart, that person voices wisdom in all areas of life, ensuring success and making certain he or she will not fall.

GOD'S WORD IS NEAR YOU

In chapter 10 of Romans, Paul gives us one of Christianity's most revered passages. In fact, it's this passage from Paul's letter to the early Roman church that has led many religious writers over the centuries to subtitle Christianity "the great confession."

Let's briefly examine these verses from Paul's letter and compare them with what we know about our spiritual voice. In many ways, Paul's words in Romans summarize everything we've discussed together in this chapter and throughout this book.

Under the inspiration of the Holy Spirit, here is what Paul wrote and proclaimed:

> Moses describes in this way the righteousness that
> is by the law: "The man who does these things will
> live by them."

> But the righteousness that is by faith says: "Do not say in your heart, 'Who will ascend into heaven?'" (that is, to bring Christ down) "or 'Who will descend into the deep?'" (that is, to bring Christ up from the dead).
>
> But what does it say? "The word is near you; it is in your mouth and in your heart," that is, the word of faith we are proclaiming: That if you confess with your mouth, "Jesus is Lord," and believe in your heart that God raised him from the dead, you will be saved.
>
> For it is with your heart that you believe and are justified, and it is with your mouth that you confess and are saved. (Rom. 10:5-10)

What Paul described here is our pathway to salvation and rebirth through faith in Jesus Christ. Unlike the external rules, regulations, and animal sacrifices of the Old Testament's Mosaic law (which acted only to cover the sins of men and women on a temporary basis), our eternal gift of forgiveness and acceptance before God came through the sacrifice of Jesus Christ on the cross. This is the divine gift that has been made available to everyone.

The gift cannot be earned. We receive it only by faith—by believing with our heart and declaring with our mouth what Christ has done for us. Our own works, efforts, and achievements will not buy it or ever grasp it. It's the pure and unparalleled gift of God and Christ.

"For it is by grace you have been saved, through faith—and this not from yourselves, it is the gift of God—not by works, so that no one can boast" (Eph. 2:8-9).

This gift of salvation is often referred to in the Bible as the gift of righteousness. It's a term that can be confusing at first, especially since we don't commonly use this word in our everyday conversations.

One of the best ways to define righteousness is to equate it with our standing before God, our "right standing" before him. Through faith in Jesus Christ, we have been reconciled with God. We are no longer God's enemies or at odds with his kingdom. With our "right standing" as Christians, we may freely and at all times approach God as the honored members of his holy family.

No angel, demon, person, or principality may ever stop us or prevent us from enjoying this personal relationship with our God. Before heaven and earth, God has made, declared, and sealed us as righteous, and this gifted status comes with the eternal benefits of his glorious kingdom.

As Paul tells us in Rom. 3:21-24:

> But now a righteousness from God, apart from law, has been made known . . . This righteousness from God comes through faith in Jesus Christ to all who believe. There is no difference, for all have sinned and fall short of the glory of God, and are justified freely by his grace through the redemption that came by Christ Jesus.

We are the "righteousness of God" because Christ paid the high price for each of us. "God made [Jesus Christ] who had no sin to be sin for us, so that in him we might become the righteousness of God" (2 Cor. 5:21).

In Your Heart and in Your Mouth

What else did Paul explain about faith in Romans chapter 10? What other key principle stands out in Paul's writings here?

Look again at verse 8: "But what does it say? 'The word is near you; it is in your mouth and in your heart,' that is, the word of faith we are proclaiming."

Paul was teaching and preaching about the belief of our heart and the words of our mouth. Yes, he was outlining and emphasizing the "I believe, therefore I speak" model of faith in action. Our voice of faith!

Look also at verse 9 where Paul wrote that "if you confess with your mouth, 'Jesus is Lord,' and believe in your heart that God raised him from the dead, you will be saved."

With our heart and mouth working together, we receive all God's promises, including his gift of salvation. To receive by faith, this is what's required of every man and woman. "For it is *with your heart that you believe* . . . and it is *with your mouth you confess*" (Rom. 10:10).

Notice one other feature of Paul's writings in Romans: He used the phrase "confess with the mouth" several times rather than our more familiar words of speaking, voicing, or expressing. What was Paul getting at?

Though we generally associate confession with the act or idea of confessing sin before God, the primary dictionary definition for the verb "confess" is "to declare faith in or adherence to," "to agree with or assent to," "to profess."

In other words, confessing is about speaking outwardly what we believe inwardly. When we confess a belief that we hold, we declare our agreement with that inner truth. We are expressing to the outside world an inward belief of our heart.

So the confession of faith is simply another great way of describing what we've been discussing throughout this book: our heart and mouth working together to express and receive God's promises.

WALKING TODAY IN YOUR NEW LIFE

As Christians, we each have been given hundreds of invaluable promises from God, each carrying his certain and abundant blessings for our life. The Bible lists them in exquisite detail, all part of our birthright in Christ. The gifts of salvation and righteousness touch only the surface of our new life in Christ.

With our new life and God beside us, no longer are we bound by earthly thinking. No longer is the status quo our accepted fate. Today, for you and for me, there's a new way and an unlimited source to meet our needs, address our concerns, and prosper our families.

But make no mistake: If we're going to walk in the fullness of all we've been given, we must be willing to search out God's promises in our Bible and store them as treasures in our heart. Then we must be willing to voice these truths over our circumstances. Remaining silent won't change our life for the better. To enjoy all the Father and the Son have set before us, we need to speak up. We each must open our big, bold, beautiful mouth to receive heaven's best for our life.

How then do we conclude this chapter? What shall we say?

Our conclusion and final response must be exactly what Paul taught us:

> The word of God is near me; it is in my heart and in my mouth—that is the word of faith I speak. To all my problems, issues, needs, and concerns, I speak the truth of God's promises this day.

> The word of God expressed from my heart and willing mouth carries the undefeatable power of his kingdom to solve my problems, supply my needs, and accomplish heaven's goals for my life.

Personal Reflections

If I give a voice—if I open my spiritual mouth—to speak God's words into my life, supernatural things happen: mountains move, my circumstances change, and my life benefits and advances.

God's words with his promised results are always near me; I keep them in my heart and express them with my mouth. These are the faith-filled words that transform my life and everything around me.

8

How to Express God's Word: Some Examples

"Our faith must move our mouth before it will move our mountain."

—*Mark Hankins*

To learn how to master anything takes practice—the roll-up-your-sleeves, hands-on, let's-get-it-started kind of practice. There's no other way. Without this approach, we never get started; we never get moving; we never achieve our goals. At best, we may become theorists or armchair quarterbacks; most often, however, we lose sight of our path completely.

So let's get started. Through a series of examples, I will show you how to construct the expressions of faith that will move mountains in your life. I will teach you how to become confident speakers, men and women who know how to release your faith through words. By example and practice, my goal is to show you how easy it is to turn on the faucet of God's power and blessings for a prosperous life.

Before we jump in, however, it's important to emphasize that the examples provided in this chapter are only that—examples. They are here as a learning tool.

My goal is not to suggest, let alone create, rigid or legalistic templates that bridle your spiritual voice. God has made each of us unique, with different personalities, distinctive talents, and individual gifts. Our spiritual voice will, and definitely must, be a reflection of these wonderful differences. After all, that's what God's kingdom is all about: a kingdom filled with freedom, love, joy, and unlimited creativity for everyone.

So learn from the examples in this chapter but then tailor what you learn to your own personality, creativity, and uniqueness. Add your heart to what you express. Stamp your signature on it all.

In the end, the only template that must guide your spiritual voice is the underlying truth of God's Word. That's your sound guide and firm boundary. By keeping your focus and attention on God's Word, you will always stay balanced and avoid the risk of wandering off into deceptive and unproductive extremes.

GOD'S PLAN, PURPOSE, AND VICTORY ARE YOURS

Putting your faith into words isn't complicated. Expressing even one of God's promises from your heart and mouth can revolutionize your life forever.

Let me share with you an example from the life of a woman who came to me for counseling when the pressures of her management job at a large corporation became unbearable. Like so many in the corporate world, she had to deal with difficult bosses, long hours, tight budgets, and problematic employees. To use her words, she was literally "the meat in the middle" of a highly compressed sandwich. She needed help—the kind of help God specializes in.

After teaching her the basic principles of putting faith into action, I led her to two of my favorite Scriptures:

The first was Proverbs 21:30 where the spirit of God proclaims, "There is no wisdom, no insight, no plan that can succeed against the Lord."

In my counseling with her, we talked about what this verse meant for her life and circumstances. We explored these words of Scripture in the light of God's unlimited goodness, power, and wisdom. We talked about God as our loving Father and our source for help, support, and blessings. We reflected on God's assertion that he would never be outwitted or outsmarted, not by men, women or by the devil himself.

The woman agreed to meditate and reflect on God's promise from Prov. 21:30. I knew that if she could grab hold of this promise, she would be able to move the many mountains plaguing her professional life.

The second Scripture I led her to was Proverbs 21:31: "The horse is made ready for the day of battle, but victory rests with the Lord."

In this verse, God again talks about the challenges of life. Our role in these challenges is to make our "horse ready for battle" by preparing diligently, working ethically, and performing in good faith the responsibilities related to our family and job. From there, however, God takes on the bigger role and the larger responsibility to ensure our success. Our victory ultimately rests in his hands.

For Christians, we have a higher source in life. We have a God who sits enthroned above the earth. We don't have to fret about what schemes, plans, and intrigues people may devise or pursue against us. God Almighty is our source, our provider, our protector. He holds our victory.

After several weeks of reflecting and meditating on these two verses, the woman began to speak the following words of faith into her life:

> There is no wisdom, no insight, no plan that can succeed against the Lord. He reigns above any plan, purpose, or scheme that people may pursue. He guarantees me justice, victory, and success in all that I do. I put my trust in him.

Each day, she would express this trust. The more the problems and concerns of her job grew, the more she spoke these bold words. Even in the quiet moments of her prayer life, she would remind the Lord of her trust in his promises.

The woman also began to express her trust through her daily attitude. Rather than constantly grumbling and complaining about what was wrong in the workplace, she began to express an attitude that was positive, hopeful, and helpful, knowing in her heart that God was in charge and that he would usher in the needed changes in his perfect timing.

She also expressed her trust in God's promises through her work ethic. She made her horse ready for battle by working diligently, acting conscientiously, and doing all she knew to advance the people and projects around her.

She did her part and, true to his word, God did his part. He began to move with goodness, power, and wisdom in all her circumstances. Things began to change—not overnight but as the weeks and months passed. For example, people in several key positions either left the company or were transferred to other departments. Other employees became more open and accepting of the woman's counsel and guidance, and their performance improved. New projects and programs were introduced and ultimately became successful. Even crucial funding needs were met, often through an unexpected chain of events.

Again, it took time, but the woman saw God's mighty hand move in her life. In the end, she advanced and was successful, as was her department and the company.

These same plans, purposes, and victories are available for each of us. God doesn't want you to be stressed out over office politics, the whims of your bosses, potential layoffs, or any other problems and concerns that the rest of the world cringes and obsesses about each waking moment. God wants you to live a life of peace, joy, and confidence, knowing that he is watching out for you and making your way successful.

God's Strength, Energy, and Creativity Are Available to You Each Day

We are a living extension of Jesus Christ. He is the vine; we are his branches. This union with Jesus includes our union with the Father—one inseparable bond that carries strength, provisions, and nourishment from them to us.

Paul learned about the importance of this union throughout the course of his life and ministry. He learned that God the Father and God the Son were the source of his strength, support, and sufficiency. They were the power that sustained him and all his efforts.

Paul taught this truth to the early churches by telling them that he had learned "the secret" of how to overcome all obstacles. Paul called it "the secret of facing every situation":

> I have strength for all things in Christ Who empowers me—I am ready for anything and equal to anything through Him Who infuses inner strength into me,

[that is, I am self-sufficient in Christ's sufficiency]. (Phil. 4:13 AMP)

Paul's message of God's strength, support, and sufficiency is a truth that David also voiced throughout his life:

> For who is God besides the Lord? And who is the Rock except our God? It is God who arms me with strength and makes my way perfect.
>
> He makes my feet like the feet of deer; he enables me to stand on the heights. He trains my hands for battle; my arms can bend a bow of bronze. (Ps. 18:31-34)

Each day David expressed his trust in God. Every morning he sang about the Lord's power and strength that accompanied him. "You give me your shield of victory, and your right hand sustains me; you stoop down to make me great," sang David before the Lord (Ps. 18:35). Like Paul, he understood the secret to overcoming all of life's challenges.

Recognize, too, that the strength and support of God and Jesus Christ include their creativity, wisdom, and insights. These resources flow out from them and are available to each of us for our career, projects, and family.

"I will instruct you and teach you in the way you should go; I will counsel you and watch over you," God plainly promises us in Psalm 32:8.

In today's world, with its ever-increasing demands for new ideas, innovative solutions, and out-of-the-box approaches, heaven's counsel is what we need more than ever. This is the creativity and the ingenuity—the "genius"—that we desperately need for modern-day living. By faith, thankfully, we have access to it all.

Constructing Your Expression of Faith

In the light of our union and in the brilliance of God's promises to us, let's construct an expression of faith to speak over our life. Each day, you and I can turn on the faucet of God's strength, support, and creativity by boldly declaring:

> I believe God's power and grace are flowing in my life. They are:
> - strengthening me in spirit, mind, and body;
> - blessing me with great patience, energy, and endurance;
> - allowing me to stand firm and not be discouraged; and
> - enabling me to face any challenge and overcome every obstacle.

Or perhaps these words of faith better express your trust in God's promises to you:

> God has armed me with strength. My feet are fast and nimble; my legs sure and strong. I can stand on heights and not fall. My hands are trained for any battle, and my arms can bend the mightiest bow.

Or consider the following expression as a way to release heaven's unlimited resources for your job, family, and goals:

> I am a living extension of the Father and the Son; they are my source and my strength. I am an inseparable part of them, and they are an inseparable part of me.

> Today, I speak their creativity, insights, and energy into my day, job, projects, and life.

I have new ideas and solutions to accomplish all that
is before me. Nothing is impossible or outside my
reach today because the grand Creator and his Son,
the maker of all things, live with me and in me.

Then again, some may want to cut to the chase by voicing Paul's
great statement of faith from Phil. 4:13: "I can do all things through
Christ who strengthens me".

Ultimately, the words you decide to use are up to you. Let the
freedom you have in God's kingdom unbridle your spiritual voice
so your words reflect your uniqueness. Express God's promises with
words that come from your heart, not necessarily mine or someone
else's.

That being said, I do encourage you to use and learn from the
expressions of faith in this chapter and throughout this book. In
the beginning, we all need good reference points to guide us; that's
why these examples are here. Use them. Speak them. Employ them
in your life. Then, as you move forward and find your own special
voice, make the changes and adjustments that fit you.

Let me also clarify another important point here so there's no
misunderstanding my advice and guidance about when to start
speaking. Start speaking God's promises now, today. Even if your
mouth may be getting ahead of your heart, that's OK—start speaking
God's promises over your life. Eventually, your heart will catch up
and grasp all that your mouth is saying.

Remember it takes time to grow God's Word within us. No matter
how rich or fertilized the soil of our heart may be, a harvestable
product doesn't appear overnight. Only with time and in due season
does the harvest come.

Plus, we're all different. A promise you might grasp quickly may
take me much longer. That's natural. I can assure you that there are

promises in God's Word that took me weeks, months, and even years before they fully sunk in. Some still haven't sunken in. Like every Christian, I'm still growing.

In the end, what will determine your success and my success in the expression of God's promises is willingness. We must be willing to start speaking.

If you're willing to start speaking the words of God's promises over your life, no matter how awkward or foreign those words might seem to you in the beginning, eventually your heart will catch up to your mouth. Eventually, God's promises will sink in and become genuine for you. With time and focus and through repeated verbalization, God's words will become your words, the authentic and sincere expression of your own heart.

Go back again to the wisdom God shared with us about how to internalize his Word. "Verbalize to internalize" was important wisdom he shared with us. He told us that our speaking and hearing would be a catalyst for us to take ownership of all his promises.

So don't wait. Start speaking God's promises. Each day, these spoken truths will chip away at any negative thoughts, beliefs, or perceptions you might harbor about your life's journey. Before long, God's words will become your words, the certain expression of your heart.

Through patience, persistence, and growing faith, you can become like George Washington Carver who, though born a slave in the old South, overcame his impoverished beginnings to become one of America's great scientists, inventors, and educators. Through God's genius, Carver unlocked the many secrets of the peanut plant, discovering more than three hundred uses for a plant considered by many to be of little value.

Whenever people asked Carver about his creative ideas and new inventions, Carver made his answer clear to them by saying, "God gave them to me. Without God to draw aside the curtain, I would be helpless."

Even today, Carver is remembered as "God's scientist."

FINANCIAL PROSPERITY IS AN INTEGRAL PART OF YOUR CHRISTIAN INHERITANCE

In God's covenant with Abraham, God promised to bless him in every way, including the blessing of financial prosperity.

Over the course of Abraham's life, God fulfilled his covenant promise. The Bible specifically tells us that "Abraham [became] very wealthy in livestock and in silver and gold" (Gen. 13:2). In fact, Abraham became so wealthy and his possessions so great that he and his nephew Lot were forced to part company as one common land could no longer support them both (Gen. 13:6).

It was obvious even to outsiders that God was with Abraham, strengthening, prospering, and guiding him. "God is with you in everything you do," they continually told Abraham, with deep respect (Gen. 21:22). They were in awe of what God was doing in Abraham's life.

When Abraham reached old age, the Bible confirms that "the Lord had blessed him in every way" (Gen. 24:1).

Of course, God's covenant of blessing was not just for Abraham but also for Abraham's descendants—the entire nation of Israel. "Blessed is the nation whose God is the Lord, the people he chose for his inheritance," declares Ps. 33:12.

In his statements to the people of Israel, God made it clear to them that they were to be blessed above all the people of the earth. In every way—spiritually, physically, emotionally, and materially—they were to prosper and succeed.

"You [God's family of chosen people] will be blessed more than any other people," God told them again and again (Deut. 7:14).

But why is God's promise to Abraham and his descendants important to us? What relevance does this promise have for Christianity?

The answer, of course, is that God's promise belongs also to us—to every Christian. We've been included in the covenant of blessing that God first announced to Abraham so many years ago. It's one of the great promises we inherited through faith in Jesus Christ.

By accepting Jesus as our Lord and Savior, we become sons and daughters of God, full heirs and proud members of his royal family. Together with the descendants of Abraham, we are now part of God's chosen people and rightful partakers of all his blessings. That's who we are and what we hold today. That's our precious standing in Christ.

Given our standing, God repeatedly refers to Christians in the New Testament as "the children of Abraham"—the spiritual children of Abraham—and therefore blessed along with Abraham and his natural line of descendants.

"Understand, then, that those who believe are children of Abraham" (Gal. 3:7). "If you belong to Christ, then you are Abraham's seed, and heirs according to the promise" (Gal. 3:29).

The bottom line: A secure future filled with prosperity and abundance belongs to every Christian. This is what we can and should expect for our life. We have God's word on it.

In our receiving, the only thing God doesn't want is for us to become selfish. His promise of prosperity and abundance carries with it the intention that we share our good fortune with others.

"You will be made rich in every way, so that you can be generous on every occasion," explained Paul (2 Cor. 9:11).

To reinforce this important message of generosity, God tells us that the more we give, the more we will receive. This is the principle of sowing and reaping that God has instituted for everyone in his family.

"Remember this: Whoever sows sparingly will also reap sparingly, and whoever sows generously will also reap generously" (2 Cor. 9:6).

God's promise of prosperity is directly linked to the principle of sowing and reaping. God wants his family to be not only the most prosperous and richly blessed people on the earth but also the most generous givers.

CONSTRUCTING YOUR EXPRESSION OF FAITH

Study these Scriptures on prosperity. Meditate on them. Internalize these truths God has shared with us for a prosperous life. Store them as treasure in your heart.

Then begin to express these truths in words—from your own spiritual "mouth." Your words of expression might look something like this:

> I am a child of God, an heir of God, a member of his royal family. Like Abraham, Isaac, and all of God's people, I am blessed by my Father with prosperity and great abundance.

> I walk in my Father's blessings today and tomorrow. This is what God has for me; this is what I expect for my life and my family; and this is what I declare over my life.

> I am prospered so I can be a generous giver to all who are in need and to all who call on me for help.

Or perhaps your expression of faith might take an approach as simple and straightforward as this: Get up in morning, look in the mirror, and declare, "I'm blessed! I'm genuinely and outrageously blessed!" You might even add, "Just like father Abraham, God is with me in everything I do!"

Whatever words you finally decide on, speak them. Take God's promise of prosperity from the reservoir of your heart and express it in your life.

Of course, your expression of faith shouldn't consist only of words. We give voice to God's promises not only through words but also through deeds. So begin expressing your faith in God's promise of prosperity by giving generously of yourself to all those who are in need. Give generously of your money, time, and talents.

Make it a point to give something of yourself each day to the people around you and to those whom God has put in your path. Provide generously for your church, those in the missionary field, and the Christian ministries God has placed on your heart. With the measure you use, so shall it be magnified back to you many times over.

Give from your heart in all that you do and in all that you say, and you will be blessed, refreshed, and prosper in every way.

FEAR, PHOBIA, AND ANXIETY HAVE NO CONTROL OVER YOU

The actress Brigitte Bardot once said, "Solitude scares me. It makes me think about love, death, and war. I need distraction from anxious, black thoughts."

Bardot's words pretty much sum up the sentiment of much of the world today. Young and old, rich and poor, people everywhere are struggling with the darkness of fear, phobia, and anxiety. Though they search out distractions of every kind—be it drugs, alcohol, sex, work, or all-consuming hobbies—they find this black cloud of fear is never far behind them, always gaining ground, always reaching out for them.

In the end, how can they outrun this black cloud? Alone, they can't, for it is Satan's plan for every man and woman. By fear and every imaginable form of anxiety, he runs his dark kingdom with an iron fist, enslaving all who are part of it. In his domain, there is no freedom, lasting joy, or inner peace.

All medical science can do in response is dream up more and more extravagant labels to describe people's fears and phobias. At times, if medical science gets especially lucky, those in the field may discover another costly drug to temporarily mask people's inner turmoil. Yet the underlying problem remains. Satan's destructive cycle of fear and anxiety continues—one endless cycle of life that isn't life.

Thankfully, there is one answer to mankind's dilemma: Jesus Christ. He came to free us from Satan's dark dominion and bring us into the kingdom of the light, God's glorious kingdom. "I have come into the world as light," said Jesus, "so that no one who believes in me should stay in darkness" (John 12:46).

Jesus came to earth for us. That was his mission. Despite the agony and unthinkable pain he would have to endure on the cross, Jesus knew that this was the only plan that would free us and allow us to live a true, full, and complete life.

Through Jesus Christ's gift of sacrifice and by his resurrection from the dead, we who believe now "share in the inheritance of the saints in the kingdom of the light" (Col. 1:12-13). We have been rescued from the dark hand of Satan forever. Fear no longer holds the right to govern or control us. In our new kingdom, only the love and light of God and Christ hold rightful dominion.

And the good news doesn't stop here. God designed a rescue plan for us that includes another revolutionary gift. It's a gift so remarkable and revolutionary that it's almost unimaginable: the gift of a new spirit! A new and invincible spirit!

Yes, to complete his plan, God has given each of us a new spirit, one that holds the power and divine presence of his Spirit—the Holy Spirit.

In his letters to the early churches, Paul continually wrote about this extraordinary gift given to believers. He told the men and women, "You did not receive a spirit that makes you a slave again to fear," but you received the unconquerable spirit of God (Rom. 8:15). God's spirit living in your spirit, Paul explained, is what supports and directs your life now.

Paul emphasized the same dramatic point to Timothy by telling him, "For God did not give us a spirit of timidity—of cowardice, of craven and cringing and fawning fear—but He has given us a spirit of power and of love and of calm and well-balanced mind and discipline and self-control" (2 Tim. 1:7 AMP).

Inside every believer today lives the heart of a champion—a spirit of invincible power, unfailing love, and complete self-control. This is who we are today. Fear is no longer our master; anxiety, depression, and phobias have no legitimate right to control us.

CONSTRUCTING YOUR EXPRESSION OF FAITH

As members and champions in a new kingdom, it's time for each of us to speak against the fears that encroach on our life. Through words of faith, it's time for us to pull the sword of the spirit from our scabbard and destroy these dreadful and irrational fears.

From out of our big, bold, beautiful mouth, we can and must speak the words of freedom:

> Fear, I come against you with the sword of the spirit, which is the word of God, the truth of God. I am a child of the light, a child of God, a member of that one true kingdom. I am no longer under your control or subject to your dark grip.

> Fear, you have no rights over my life. I come against you in the name and in the power of God Almighty and the Lord Jesus Christ. I break your hold, and I demand you step aside.

Or consider the following faith-filled words to destroy any dark images or anxieties that seek to oppress you:

> Fear, anxiety, depression, I come against you and I demolish your plan, purpose, and intent for my life. I give you no place here.

> You are of the devil, not of God. I know this because I have God's spirit living in me, a spirit of invincible power, unfailing love, and complete self-control. God's spirit in me is what controls and directs every moment of my life.

Fight back with the truth. Take the sword of the spirit—the word of God sown in your heart—and put that supernatural sword into action. Speak up! Demand your rights! Don't settle for anything less!

BE WILLING TO FIND AND THEN SPEAK

With God's Word treasured in your heart and with a wide-open mouth, you can revolutionize your life and circumstances. From the examples in this chapter, you can see that it's not difficult or complicated. Nothing from God ever is.

More than anything else, what's needed from us to succeed is willingness. We must be willing to find out what God has promised us in the Bible, and, from there, we must be willing to speak.

Finding God's promises is always our first step. It's the reason every example in this chapter began by first focusing on God's Word. What did God's Word say about our concern? What wisdom did God record for our benefit? What did he ask us to believe?

When we know what God's Word promises us, we have a secure and trustworthy guide. With the understanding of his Word, we have a tangible truth that our heart can grab onto for victory.

From there, it comes down to speaking—to opening our mouth to release and enjoy God's countless blessings. If we're willing to take this second strategic step, nothing is beyond our reach. Everything is possible.

Personal Reflections

With God's Word treasured in my heart and with a wide-open mouth, I can revolutionize my life and my circumstances.

When my faith moves my mouth, every mountain and obstacle before me must move aside.

PART III

THE COMMAND OF FAITH:

COMMANDING EXPRESSION

9

Just Give the Command:
Understanding Your Authority

"Oh while I live, to be the ruler of life, not a slave, to meet life as a powerful conqueror, and nothing exterior to me will ever take command of me."

—*Walt Whitman*

"The successful cavalryman must educate himself to say 'Charge!'"

—*George S. Patton*

Our journey to understanding the depth and breadth of our spiritual expression brings us to another door. It's a door inscribed with the words "Christian authority" to highlight the foundation on which it stands and the acknowledgement of all those who are called to enter. This door marks an important passage, one created for every Christian to walk through.

When you and I venture through this door, we find ourselves looking out across the vast landscape of God's kingdom. The hills, valleys, and rooftops stretch out before us in almost unimaginable proportions. We see dazzling colors and the never-ending majesty of the heavenly kingdom.

From this lofty vantage point, we see even more clearly what it means to be a Christian—who we are, what we're part of, and what we've been given. We see our unlimited potential and breathtaking empowerment. We see our heritage as members of God's family and our role as Christ's representatives in the earth. We see it all.

From this vantage point, we also recognize, perhaps like never before, that we've been given authority by God and Christ to speak special words: the words of faith's commands. With these bold words, we realize that the obstacles and forces that seek to block, limit, and defeat us must submit because the power of God's kingdom—our kingdom—is standing with us, always there to back up our commands.

Through this door and on this high vista, we reach a natural progression in our journey into faith's expressions. We reach a place of added expertise and mature insight. We reach the place where our spiritual voice is confident and results certain.

So let's continue our journey together and walk through this wonderful door.

JESUS AND THE ROMAN CENTURION

The gospels of Matthew and Luke recorded the real-life drama of Jesus and the Roman centurion. This inspiring and instructional story provides the backdrop for many of our lessons in Part III of this book. Surprisingly, it's a very short story, one that begins with a great and pressing need:

The Roman centurion paced the floor as his beloved servant lay paralyzed and near death. The dying man, the centurion's dear friend, needed the kind of help that only God could offer.

As the centurion paced, the man people called Jesus tugged relentlessly on his heart. He had heard the stories about this man, this Jesus. People were calling him God's man of miracles and the person who turned around impossible situations.

As the centurion paced, those words and stories consumed him. With every measured step, he realized more clearly that Jesus was the one he needed to call on for help. He needed this man of God's miracles.

But would Jesus help? Would he respond to a centurion's call? It was a bold request, especially given the highly charged environment of the day. He was asking Jesus, a Jew, to intercede on behalf of a non-Jew—and a Roman military officer no less. His aides told him it was an absurd request.

Absurd, perhaps, but not to Jesus. Jesus had come to earth for every desperate person and every impossible situation. Yes, Jesus would come. He would help. And he would bring God's divine power to advance God's promised blessings for all mankind.

On hearing the news, the centurion was overjoyed, but one concern still troubled him deeply. Humbly, respectfully, and with absolute sincerity, he expressed his concern to Jesus, saying, "Lord, I do not deserve to have you come under my roof. But just say the word, and my servant will be healed" (Matt. 8:8).

Astonishing! The centurion wasn't asking Jesus to make a personal visit to his home. Rather, his only request was that Jesus issue a command. Jesus, just say the word—just give the command. For the centurion, Jesus' command was more than sufficient to heal his dying servant.

The centurion's request and the maturity of his faith delighted Jesus. Jesus called it a high-water mark for faith that day. "I tell you the truth, I have not found anyone in Israel with such great faith," said Jesus to all his disciples (Matt. 8:10).

Of course, you know what happened next. Jesus gave the command: "Go! It will be done just as you believed it would" (Matt. 8:13). As that pronouncement left Jesus' lips, the Bible tells us that the centurion's servant was healed at that exact moment.

UNDERSTANDING AUTHORITY

So what was at work here? What did the Roman centurion understand and believe about the situation at hand? What moved this man to ask for a single command to be spoken for the miraculous to take place in his life?

The answers are actually very simple. First, the Roman centurion understood the principle we call authority. He understood what authority is, how it works, and how effective it is for achieving results in any kingdom, both earthly and heavenly.

In five short sentences, the centurion explained the principle of authority like this:

> Lord, I do not deserve to have you come under my roof. But just say the word, and my servant will be healed. For I myself am a man under authority, with soldiers under me. I tell this one, "Go," and he goes; and that one, "Come," and he comes. I say to my servant, "Do this," and he does it. (Matt. 8:8-9)

The centurion was an agent of Rome, an official representative of the Roman empire—a commander with one hundred soldiers underneath him. He was, in his words, "a man under authority, with soldiers under him." It was that authority—the authority entrusted to him by Rome—that gave him the official right to control and direct the resources and fighting men of Rome.

What else did our centurion understand? Just as importantly, he understood that authority is primarily exercised through the issuance of commands. That's how authority speaks. "I tell this one, 'Go,' and he goes; and that one, 'Come,' and he comes. I say to my servant, 'Do this,' and he does it." Those are the words—"Go," "Come," "Do this"—that set into motion the actions and forces that accomplish the goals of any kingdom.

From years of military experience, the centurion understood the principle of authority. Without question, he understood his right to speak the orders and commands that would marshal Roman power and alter the earthly landscapes around him.

When we stop to consider the principle of authority described by the Roman centurion, doesn't his explanation ring true based on our own experiences? Wouldn't you agree that his comments accurately describe how authority operates even in our modern workplaces and present-day societies?

Sure, I think we all would agree. But before we nod our final agreement, let's confirm our understanding with a short exercise:

In your dictionary, look up the word authority. I think you'll be pleasantly surprised by what you find. In my dictionary, authority is specifically defined as "the right to issue orders and commands" or "the legal or official right to command thought, opinion, or behavior."

Also look up the definition of the word command—more specifically the verb. In my dictionary, the verb command means "to exercise direct authority."

By modern definition, commands and orders go hand in hand with authority. They work together; they're inseparably linked. The Roman centurion was spot on with his wisdom and understanding. He was "a commander of Rome" for very good reason, as that's how authority is primarily exercised.

THE ESSENTIAL ELEMENT OF FAITH

Of course, understanding how authority works wasn't the only element that prompted the Roman centurion to ask for Jesus' command. The other critical element was his belief that Jesus was God's representative on the earth. In his heart, the centurion firmly believed that Jesus was entrusted with the authority of the heavenly kingdom.

Without this added element of faith, the centurion would not have received his answer. His faith was essential. As Jesus explained to him, "It will be done just as you believed it would" (Matt. 8:13). The centurion's faith completed the circuit necessary for his miraculous answer.

The story of Jesus and the Roman centurion is an important lesson. By understanding the basic insights of this story, we equip ourselves with the principles of authority and the words of command that go with it. This story also confirms the essential ingredient of faith, which must accompany all our words, requests, and other actions.

RECOGNIZING THE EXERCISE OF AUTHORITY

There were others in Israel who recognized Jesus' exercise of authority as he went about healing the sick and performing God's miracles.

In the town of Capernaum, for example, a crowd of people carrying a paralytic man on a stretcher asked for Jesus' help.

When Jesus approached the stretcher, the crowd watched intently to see what would happen. Would Jesus pray for the paralyzed man? Would he lay his hands on him? Would he prepare some special medicine?

To everyone's surprise, Jesus opened his mouth and spoke a healing command: "Get up, take your mat and go home" (Matt. 9:6). Immediately, the paralytic man did just that, he got up and went home.

The crowd marveled at Jesus' authority—how Jesus spoke the command and the man was healed. "When the crowd saw this, they were filled with awe; and they praised God, who had given such authority to men" (Matt. 9:8). They recognized that God had given Jesus the authority to command the miraculous, and they thanked God for it.

In Luke chapter 4, we find a similar example. Here Jesus encountered a demon-possessed man in the synagogue. When the demon cried out, Jesus quickly responded by ordering the demon to shut up and leave the man. "Be quiet! Come out of him!" commanded Jesus (Luke 4:35).

The order having been given, the demon had no choice but to go. "The demon threw the man down before them all and came out without injuring him" (Luke 4:35).

The crowd was stunned by the exercise of authority they had just witnessed. "All the people were amazed and said to each other, 'What is this teaching? With authority and power he gives orders to evil spirits and they come out!'" (Luke 4:36).

Of course, it wasn't just the laity who recognized Jesus' authority as he went about healing the sick and ministering to those in need; the chief priests, Pharisees, and leaders of the temple recognized it as well. Schooled in the principles of authority, they wanted to know much more about Jesus.

They would constantly prod Jesus, asking him, "By what authority are you doing these things? And who gave you this authority?" (Matt. 21:23).

Jesus, tell us who is empowering you? Who gave you the authority that allows you to issue these healing orders and these miraculous commands? What kingdom is standing behind you and your words?

With their questions, they were looking for ways to discredit Jesus. They wanted to show that it wasn't God's kingdom empowering Jesus but rather Satan's demonic kingdom. At every turn, they would incite the people of Israel by falsely telling them, "It is only by Beelzebub, the prince of demons, that this fellow [Jesus] drives out demons" (Matt. 12:24).

WHOSE GOALS ARE BEING ACCOMPLISHED?

Jesus' response to the false accusations about him centered on one key question: Whose kingdom, God's or Satan's, am I benefiting by what I'm doing? That was Jesus' rebuttal to his accusers.

Jesus formed the question to his accusers like this: "Every kingdom divided against itself will be ruined, and every city or household divided against itself will not stand. If Satan drives out Satan, he is divided against himself. How then can his kingdom stand?" (Matt. 12:25-26).

Let me paraphrase Jesus' words to clarify his argument to the Jewish leadership: "If I'm destroying Satan's goals by healing the sick and helping those in need, then certainly I can't be an agent of Satan's demonic kingdom. To do so, I'd be dividing and destroying the very kingdom you accuse me of representing and supporting."

Jesus would then carry his argument to its logical and final conclusion by saying to his accusers, "But if I drive out demons by the Spirit of God, then the kingdom of God has come upon you" (Matt. 12:28).

Jesus' final comment was piercing. He was telling the chief priests, Pharisees, and leaders of Israel to wake up and admit the truth of what was going on around them.

In modern-day language, Jesus was saying to them: "Be honest, gentlemen, what you are seeing and experiencing before your very own eyes is the kingdom of God in action for your benefit and the benefit of all your people. It's God's power—the spirit of God—at work. That's the kingdom backing up my words, my commands, and all my actions. So wake up, and stop lying about who I represent!"

EVERY AGENT MUST BE GIVEN AUTHORITY

In the account of Jesus and his accusers, the Bible brings out one other point that's important to our understanding of authority. It's this: Every agent—both earthly and heavenly—*must* be given authority by the person or principal who appoints them.

I know "must" is a strong word here, but recognize why: The giving (or delegation) of authority is what channels the power of the principal into the hands of an agent. This transfer of authority is what empowers the agent. It's what gives the agent the right to use, access, and command the resources needed to accomplish the goals and tasks to which he or she has been assigned.

Without authority from the principal, an agent is isolated and alone. He or she is powerless. Delegated authority is the critical asset every agent in every kingdom must have to succeed and achieve.

To highlight this point further, reflect for a moment on Jesus' earthly mission as God's representative: Would God—or any employer for that matter—appoint an agent but then refuse to give that agent the authority necessary to accomplish his or her mission? Would that make sense? Would it be fair or prudent? Of course not. To do so would be irrational, irresponsible, and downright dangerous.

Consider the Roman centurion: Was he chosen to be a representative of Rome but then left stranded and alone? No, he was empowered by Caesar to command the soldiers and resources of the Roman Empire. Like Jesus, he was given kingdom authority to use.

Both common sense and prudence require that an agent be entrusted with the authority necessary to accomplish the goals for which he or she has been engaged. It's why Jesus stressed over and over to the Jewish leadership, "Whose goals am I accomplishing by what I'm doing—God's or Satan's?"

If Jesus was healing the sick and performing God's miracles among the people, then there was only one answer: He was God's representative. God, not Satan, was the principal who delegated authority to Jesus. God was the one who empowered Jesus to direct and command the miracles taking place among the people.

Let's look also in the dictionary for confirmation of the authority that must be given to those whom we appoint as our agents and representatives:

- An agent is defined as "one who acts for or in place of another *through delegated authority.*" The giving or delegation of authority is what establishes the relationship.

- A representative is defined as "one who represents another as agent, deputy, substitute, or delegate and *who is invested with the authority of the principal.*" Again, it's the delegated authority that is central to the relationship.

- Look also at the word empower, which we commonly use to describe the underlying enablement of an agent or representative. The definition of the verb empower is *"to give official authority."*

- We see the same description for the word authorize. To authorize means *"to invest with authority."* We invest, give, or delegate authority to another person whenever we authorize that person to act on our behalf.

- Another word often used to describe an agent's role or mission is the word commission. A commission is *"an authorization to act in a certain manner or to perform certain tasks."* The verb commission means *"to give or entrust authority."*

From the definitions above, we see the vital and enabling role authority plays whenever we ask someone to act on our behalf. Authority is the underlying investment every principal must make in an agent in order to allow and ensure a successful job, task, or mission.

It's no different in God's kingdom. When God selected Jesus as heaven's representative, God empowered, authorized, and commissioned Jesus to complete his mission on earth. God gave Jesus the authority necessary to do what he was called to do. God made the investment in him.

Look at what God said about Jesus and his mission to earth: "Here is my servant, whom I uphold, my chosen one in whom I delight; I will put my Spirit on him, and he will bring justice to the nations" (Isa. 42:1; see also Matt. 12:18).

THE COMMANDS JESUS ISSUED

The Bible records many of the orders and commands Jesus spoke as he went about his mission on earth. Here are a few highlights:

o "You deaf and mute spirit, I command you, come out of him and never enter him again" (Mark 9:25). This was the command Jesus gave to the demon spirit oppressing a young boy.

o "Stretch out your hand" (Matt. 12:13). This was the command Jesus issued to restore a man's shriveled and deformed hand.

o "Quiet! Be still!" (Mark 4:39). This was the order Jesus spoke to the storm that threatened to capsize the boat carrying Jesus and the disciples. Immediately upon Jesus' rebuke, the storm ceased and all became calm.

o "May no one ever eat fruit from you again" (Mark 11:14). These were the commanding words Jesus spoke to a fig tree, causing that tree to wither and die.

PROCLAMATIONS AND PRONOUNCEMENTS

When we talk about orders and commands, we sometimes use fancy words to describe them—words such as "proclamations" and "pronouncements."

We see these terms used most often in legal or government circles, as they convey an aura of formality and decorum. The terms just sound so official. When we hear them, we immediately think to ourselves, "Wow, that person called it a proclamation [or a pronouncement], so those words must be important and official."

But please don't let the formality of these terms confuse you: Proclamations and pronouncements are and always will be commands. They are words of authority spoken to announce an outcome, result, or decree.

Let me share an example to make this more clear. Do you remember the pronouncement routinely spoken by the justice of the peace in certain Hollywood movies? Do you remember what this government agent says when he marries a movie's romantic couple? I'm sure you can recite the exact words, which are still spoken by justices of the peace in California and states across America today: "By the authority vested in me by the State of California, I pronounce you husband and wife."

(Note: California is used in our example; but, of course, the applicable home state of the justice would be the one used in the pronouncement.)

Do you see how this pronouncement emphasizes the authority given to the justice of the peace to issue the decree of marriage? The words are wrapped in official garb. Yet when we look past the formality, the justice's words are still just the words of command—nothing more, nothing less.

In fact, if we go back to our dictionary one last time, we find that proclamations and pronouncements are defined simply as "authoritative announcements." And the verbs pronounce or proclaim simply mean "to declare clearly, forcefully, *and authoritatively.*"

Armed with this understanding, let's look at a few of the proclamations or pronouncements Jesus spoke by the authority vested in him by God:

o "Your request is granted." This was the pronouncement Jesus issued for the woman who asked for her daughter's healing (Matt. 15:28).

o "You may go. Your son will live." This was the pronouncement Jesus spoke when a government official asked for the healing of his gravely ill child (John 4:50).

o "Be clean!" These were the words of proclamation Jesus spoke for the healing of a man with leprosy (Matt. 8:3).

Through his commands, Jesus did what God asked of him. From demons to sickness to storms and all manner of obstacles and problems, Jesus spoke the orders, pronouncements, and proclamations that released God's power.

AND GOD SAID . . .

Isn't this the same commanding process God used to create the universe and all its wonders, mankind included?

If we open our Bible to the first page of the first chapter, we can read all about it. Over and over in the book of Genesis are the commanding pronouncements God spoke from his spiritual mouth to set everything into being:

o "And God said, 'Let there be light,' and there was light" (Gen. 1:3).

o "And God said, 'Let there be an expanse between the waters to separate water from water,'" and so it came to be (Gen. 1:6).

o "And God said, 'Let the water teem with living creatures, and let birds fly above the earth across the expanse of the sky,'" and so it was (Gen. 1: 20).

o Then God announced throughout his heavenly kingdom, "Let us make man in our image, in our likeness, and let them rule . . . over all the earth," and, from this commanding expression, man was created upon the earth and given dominion over it (Gen. 1:26).

The Bible is filled with example after example of God's spiritual commands and the results that followed. Through its pages, God has given us a spectacular showcase of his own spiritual voice in full commanding expression.

THE COMMAND OF FAITH—JESUS EXPLAINS

But what about us? What about you? What about me? How does all this talk of authority apply to us?

Jesus explained the importance in Matthew chapter 11. Here he gave us a firsthand tutorial on how we as Christians have been empowered to speak these same commands.

Jesus began his lesson with a demonstration. He announced to an unfruitful fig tree, "May no one ever eat fruit from you again" (Mark 11:13-14).

By the next morning, Peter and the other disciples saw that the fig tree had died. Astonished by what had taken place, Peter grabbed Jesus by the arm and said, "Rabbi, look! The fig tree you cursed has withered!" (Mark 11:20-21).

Peter then asked the big question: Jesus, how did this happen? What did you do here?

In response, Jesus explained to the disciples the command of faith:

> "Have faith in God," Jesus answered. "I tell you the truth, if anyone says to this mountain, 'Go throw yourself into the sea,' and does not doubt in his heart

but believes that what he says will happen, it will be done for him." (Mark 11:22-23)

I know we've touched on this Scripture from Mark's gospel in some of our earlier discussions on spiritual expression, but now it's time to crack these verses wide open and extract even more treasure.

The first treasure is our Christian empowerment. Jesus is telling us that the authority to issue faith's commands—to say to the mountain, "Go throw yourself into the sea"—is an empowerment given to every believer, not just a select few. The word anyone here means you and me, each and every Christian.

The King James' word for anyone is "whosoever." I like that old English word because it emphasizes the empowerment given to every believer. All Christians—the entire family of God—have been called, commissioned, and authorized to speak faith's commands on the earth.

What else is Jesus teaching us here? He is, of course, teaching us about faith's essential role in this supernatural process. Faith—our faith—is central to it all. Jesus even prefaces his instructions by saying, "Have faith in God." It's our personal trust in God and our heart-centered belief in God's promises that provide the unshakable foundation for us to speak.

Without faith, you and I have no foundation. Only when we trust God and believe what he has said about our union with him and Christ Jesus do we know without a doubt in our heart that we have been entrusted with authority. Only when we believe the truth of who we are and what we've been given as Christians do we fully recognize our commission to speak heaven's commands on the earth.

When we believe we are legitimate members of God's kingdom—the royal representatives, the sons and daughters of God Almighty—

then we can confidently say to our problems and concerns, "Move aside," "Go throw yourself into the sea," or "Hit the road," knowing that God's power stands behind us, backing up our orders and ensuring the final result.

When you believe in your heart that the kingdom of God and Christ is your kingdom, the idea of issuing commands and proclamations becomes normal to you. There are no lingering doubts. Commands, proclamations, and pronouncements become just another part of who you are and what you do.

With this faith, this unshakable trust, we reach the place Paul spoke about where "in all these things, we are more than conquerors through him who loved us" (Rom. 8:37). We become God's conquerors and commanders over problems and obstacles, over sickness and disease, and over every demonic power that may seek to oppress us.

By faith, this is who we are and what we've each been given. With this same faith, we can confidently say to the mountains in our life, "Go throw yourself into the sea" and "not doubt in our heart but believe" that our commands—"what we say will happen"—will happen. It will happen! It "will be done for us!"

"I Believe, Therefore I Command"

Perhaps the best way to summarize what Jesus taught us in Mark 11:22-23 is this: The command of faith is about knowing and expressing who we are as Christians. Through faith's commands, we give full voice to the divine truth of our new life in Christ. Full voice to the truth of who you are in Christ Jesus!

Viewed from this perspective, the principles of spiritual expression discussed in Mark 11 are really no different than the ones we've studied in earlier chapters. It's the same "I believe, therefore I speak" pattern of faith. The same heart and mouth working together. The same precepts of putting faith into action, turning on the faucet, externalizing our inward trust.

Sure, the focus and emphasis are slightly different. Words of command are now our focus. "I believe, therefore I command" is now the pattern of our expression. But it's still our heart and mouth functioning together. It's still God's power being released through our words—our commanding words.

With our understanding of faith's commands, we reach a special place in our journey into faith's expressions. By taking hold of our God-given authority and the words that go with it, you and I become unstoppable commanders in God's incomparable kingdom.

So grab hold and begin speaking the commands and pronouncements that define your Christian heritage:

- I believe who I am in Christ, in God's kingdom, in the family of the Father and the Son. Therefore, I speak the commands of faith that move mountains in my life.

- I believe that "God has raised [me] up with Christ and seated [me] with him in the heavenly realms" (Eph. 2:6). I believe that's my position of authority and empowerment. I believe God has made this great investment in me.

  Therefore, I speak the official orders and decrees that advance my life and my kingdom.

Recognize, believe, and begin utilizing your heavenly commission:

- I believe Jesus Christ has commissioned me as his personal representative (2 Cor. 5:20 AMP) and "enriched [me] in full power and readiness of speech to speak my faith" (1 Cor. 1:5 AMP).

- I believe I am his "living branch" on the earth today (John 15:5).

- I believe I am "Christ's ambassador, as though God were making his appeal through [me]" (2 Cor. 5:20).

  Therefore, I speak the proclamations and pronouncements that advance the plans and purposes of Jesus Christ in my life, home, and community.

Move forward today with all that you have been given:

- I believe the authorization given to me by Jesus when he declared, "All authority in heaven and on earth has been given to me. Therefore, go . . ." (Matt. 28:18-19). I believe Jesus authorized me to go on his behalf.

  Therefore, I speak the commands that go hand in hand with my calling.

Take a good look around you today and be encouraged. You're not stranded, isolated, or alone. God didn't call and commission you to be his earthly agent and powerful commander but then refuse to give you the authority you need to accomplish your goals and achieve his heavenly mission. Jesus Christ died so that every man and woman who believes in him could enter into the fullness of his life and have access to the abundant resources, divine tools, and precious support we each need to succeed on earth and in life.

Personal Reflections

I am the commander Father God and Jesus Christ have told me I am. I am the one who believes in my heart and speaks from my mouth the commands of faith that move mountains and change impossible landscapes in my life.

10

"God Bless You!": A Christian Speaks

"Before all else, we seek upon our common labor as a nation, the blessings of Almighty God."
—*Dwight D. Eisenhower*

If you and I could go back and ask any one of our Bible heroes what words best define our God-given authority and the pronouncements that go with it, their answer would be immediate: God bless you!

From prophets to kings and countless Christians in between, those three words have always highlighted our authority. From the days of Abraham and the saints of old, those were the words that enriched nations and graced innumerable lives. For our patriarchs, no better words could capture our God-given empowerment.

So what happened? What changed? Today, these words seem to go unnoticed; they no longer stand out. It's as if they've somehow faded into the background of modern-day living. They've become just another polite comment, another friendly gesture, the perfect response to an uncontrollable sneeze.

Why? Have we heard the words too often? Have we not heard them enough? Maybe we've found better words, more eloquent or effective words to utter?

No, I think not.

What then? Well, perhaps we've lost our perspective on what's being spoken, what's being transferred.

Yes, I think that's it. In all our modern pursuits and endeavors, I believe we've lost the meaning behind these three great words. The value has slipped through our fingers as we've gone searching in other directions.

Before you think I'm being critical with my comments, I'm not. Really, I'm not. Without solid teaching, it's easy to dismiss these words or pass them off as some outdated tradition. Only when we understand the principles of faith that come together in these three words do the words gain their full and lasting value.

Using Your Empowerment

"God bless you!"

I said it.

"God bless you!"

There, I said it again.

Did you notice the exclamation mark? It's there for a reason—because my statement is a pronouncement. It's an authoritative announcement. I've issued an official decree, one that carries an official outcome—all for your benefit.

Remember the example of the justice of the peace who issues the decree of marriage. The same principles of authority are at work when we declare "God bless you!" With just three words, we are saying, "By the authority vested in me by God and Christ and their heavenly kingdom, I pronounce God's blessings on you!"

It's one of Christianity's most amazing declarations, one founded on the deepest and most mature principles of our faith. Everything we've learned about our new life in Christ and our empowerment to speak faith's commands is wrapped up into these three words. Nothing is left out.

God bless you! Yes, God bless you! These are our words of authority, value, and results. When we speak them from our heart, God's kingdom springs into action with the power and resources to bring about our spoken end result.

The Mosaic Law's Priestly Blessing

To fully grasp the empowerment given to Christians to pronounce God's blessings, it's helpful to understand what these pronouncements looked like under the rules of the Old Testament's Mosaic law.

In the Old Testament, God gave Moses a long and detailed list of regulations to govern the Israelites as they passed into the Promised Land. These rules are often called the Mosaic law because God gave them to Moses as laws for the people to follow. (See the books of Exodus, Leviticus, Numbers, and Deuteronomy for a compilation of these rules and regulations).

One prominent part of the Mosaic law was God's establishment of a priesthood under the lineage of Aaron, Moses' brother. In Hebrew, the word for priest is *Kohen*; the plural is *Kohanim*. Only the direct male descendants of Aaron could become priests under this strict system of laws. No other Israelite, regardless of personal desire, was permitted to enter this holy order.

The Mosaic law also mandated that only the priests were authorized to minister in the temple and perform the other duties entrusted to them by God. God's line of authority for the priests was definite, clear, and precise. For someone who wasn't a priest, crossing that line meant the ultimate penalty: death.

Another prized responsibility entrusted to the *Kohanim* was the pronouncement of God's blessing over the assembled nation of Israel. God's instruction for this blessing is outlined in the book of Numbers:

> And the Lord said to Moses, "Say to Aaron and his sons, 'This is the way you shall bless the Israelites. Say to them,
>
> The Lord bless you, and watch, guard, and keep you;
>
> The Lord make His face to shine upon and enlighten you and be gracious (kind, merciful, and giving favor) to you;
>
> The Lord lift up His [approving] countenance upon you, and give you peace (tranquility of heart and life continually).'"
>
> "And they shall put My name upon the Israelites, and I will bless them." (Num. 6:22-27 AMP)

As God's instruction makes clear, the priests were to speak this pronouncement over the people. They were to issue this official decree of God's blessings for the nation. In return, God promised to honor those words with his divine benefits. "And I will bless them," said God.

In most Jewish synagogues today, the Mosaic law's priestly blessing is still pronounced. A meaningful debate, however, exists among Orthodox, Conservative, and Jewish Reform groups over who is qualified or authorized to give this priestly blessing.

Some groups maintain that only a male descendant of Aaron (a *Kohen*) may deliver the blessing. Others have relaxed or abandoned the requirement because of the difficulty in tracing individual ancestry directly back to Aaron and his line of descendants.

Recently, this debate was further underscored by a study undertaken by a group of Jewish researchers. Using the tools of modern science, these researchers attempted to trace and identify today's *Kohanim* through DNA testing. In their groundbreaking study, they examined the Y chromosome of Jewish men who claimed to be of *Kohanim* ancestry. The researchers wanted to find out whether any inherited genetic markers existed within this group of men.

What they found was fascinating: A distinctive genetic link did exist among a majority of men from this *Kohanim* group. The men shared inherited DNA markers not found in others.

Based on the results of their 1997 study as well as several follow-up studies, many experts now claim that a unique *Kohen* gene likely exists, one that potentially traces its root back over thousands of years!

CHRISTIANITY'S NEW GENETIC MARKERS

As interesting as the Jewish genetic studies are, thankfully, for Christians, all questions of ancestry and authority have been resolved for us. There's no need for ongoing debates or DNA testing.

Christ has opened the way for us all, male and female, young and old, Jew and gentile. He has given every Christian a new way and a new life.

"If anyone is in Christ, [they] are a new creation; the old has gone, the new has come!" (2 Cor. 5:17).

Through Christ's blood shed on the cross and our faith in him, we have each inherited his genetic markers, signature spirit, and distinctive life. We are new creations, birthed in Christ, and members now of one universal body—the body of Christ.

Again and again, the Bible confirms our transformative birth and distinctive heritage as members of the body of Christ:

- We are "a chosen people, a royal priesthood, a holy nation," Peter explained (1 Peter 2:9).

- We are "Christ's ambassadors, as though God were making his appeal through us," Paul explained (2 Cor. 5:20).

- We are "God's temple," a living temple where "God's Spirit lives in [us]" (1 Cor. 3:16).

Every Christian has received the gifts and calling of God. Every Christian has been empowered by the Father and the Son. Every Christian has been given the authority to act, speak, and declare heaven's blessings on earth.

I like how the Amplified Bible flushes out Christianity's empowerment even further by calling us "Christ's personal representatives":

> So we are Christ's ambassadors, God making His appeal as it were through us. We [as Christ's personal representatives] beg you for His sake to lay hold of

the divine favor [now offered you] and be reconciled
to God. (2 Cor. 5:20 AMP)

Today, we are Christ's personal representatives in our homes,
schools, and communities. We are heaven's ambassadors and the
Father's royal priesthood on the earth. With this commission and
through our authority, we have been entrusted with the words of
God's blessings for the world and the lives around us.

INVOKING GOD'S INTERVENTION

When we talk about the pronouncement of God's blessings, another
term often used to describe this official action is "invoke". Through
our words, we invoke the involvement and intervention of God.
With our words, we place God and his kingdom power into the lives
and circumstances of the people around us.

Weigh the enormity of what this means for you: Through three
faith-filled words—God bless you!—you guide and direct the hand
of God. This is the power and authority that God and Jesus have
entrusted to you.

To help me understand the enormity of this, I sometimes imagine
myself holding a giant fire hose, the fire hose of heaven's blessings.
Through my words of blessing, I see myself pointing a jet stream of
water toward others. In the direction of my words, I am showering
those around me with God's goodness, support, and abundance.

After a soaking like this, how can anyone's life be the same? It
can't. When God intervenes with his goodness, wisdom, and power,
life must change, improve, and advance. When God turns his face
toward us and shines his countenance on us, our world must be
illuminated with the brilliant colors of his glorious presence.

I love the way Proverbs describes God's blessing: "The blessing of the Lord, it makes [truly] rich, and He adds no sorrow with it" (Prov. 10:22 AMP).

God's blessings always enrich our lives—not just with material wealth but with true wealth. The wealth of family and friends. The wealth of health, strength, and vitality. The wealth of creativity and peace. The wealth of freedom. Qualities that make for a life worth living.

God knows our needs. He knows our dreams and individual desires. He knows what will bring us lasting happiness. And he alone has the power and the resources to make it all happen.

Notice also what Prov. 10:22 emphasizes about God's blessing: "He adds no sorrow with it." God doesn't give with one hand and then take with the other. His blessings don't come with hidden costs or a devil's bargain. When God blesses, he blesses—no strings attached.

It's the reason Isaiah said, "Whoever invokes a blessing in the land will do so by the God of truth" (Isa. 65:16). It's the same reason former president Ronald Reagan declared, "Freedom prospers only where the blessings of God are avidly sought and humbly accepted."

It's the reason the United States Supreme Court begins each day's session with the words, "God save the United States and this honorable court!"

It's also the reason Gen. Dwight D. Eisenhower, on the eve of World War II's monumental D-Day invasion, concluded his address to the nation by saying, "And let us all beseech the blessings of Almighty God upon this great and noble undertaking."

JACOB'S LIFE—THE VALUE OF GOD'S BLESSING

In the Bible, perhaps no one grasped the value of God's blessings more than Isaac's son Jacob. Jacob's life was one comprehensive lesson in the extraordinary benefits of God's blessing.

Born the youngest of twin boys, Jacob had God's hand on him from the very beginning. While he was still inside his mother's womb, God told Jacob's mother, Rebekah, that Jacob would rise above his twin brother, Esau, and become a mighty nation. That was God's call on Jacob's life.

God's wisdom for Jacob was confirmed when Esau later sold his birthright inheritance (called the *bekorah* in Hebrew) to Jacob for nothing more than a warm meal. In God's eyes, Esau's decision to squander his inheritance amounted to a "despising of his birthright" (Gen. 25:34). A "profane, godless, and sacrilegious" act was another description used in the Bible to describe Esau's squandering (Heb. 12:16 AMP).

What Esau "despised," Jacob deeply treasured. Even from a young age, Jacob appreciated the special rights and benefits that came to the firstborn son. Indeed, the Bible tells us that Jacob, while still in the womb, began his wrestle with Esau to become the firstborn son (Gen. 25:22-26).

When Esau squandered his birthright inheritance, Jacob's long pursuit was finally becoming a reality. However, there was still one last birthright treasure for Jacob to secure: the spiritual blessing of the firstborn son (called the *berakhah* in Hebrew).

Under the customs of that day, the firstborn son was entitled to receive both the *bekorah* (the larger portion of his father's estate) and the *berakhah* (the father's spiritual blessing).

With the help of Rebekah and God's consenting hand, Jacob took his father's spiritual blessing by impersonating his brother in the waning days of his father's life. Through guts, guile, and determination, Jacob obtained this final birthright treasure.

Listen to the magnificent words of blessing that Isaac pronounced over Jacob:

> When Isaac caught the smell of his clothes, he blessed him and said,
>
>> "Ah, the smell of my son is like the smell of a field that the Lord has blessed.
>>
>> May God give you of heaven's dew and of earth's richness—an abundance of grain and new wine.
>>
>> May nations serve you and peoples bow down to you. Be lord over your brothers, and may the sons of your mother bow down to you.
>>
>> May those who curse you be cursed and those who bless you be blessed." (Gen. 27:27-29)

Over the course of Jacob's life, Isaac's blessing closely followed him. When Jacob went to live with his wife's family in the Paddan Aran region, God continually helped him and allowed him to prosper. Jacob prospered even though Laban, his father-in-law, tried to cheat him at every turn.

As the months and years of Jacob's life advanced, Jacob recognized ever more clearly the priceless value of the words his father had spoken over him. With each passing season, Jacob understood more and more the unrivaled benefits of God's blessing, just as Abraham and Isaac had before him. And with these growing realizations, Jacob's faith in God deepened.

There was, however, one final struggle that lay ahead in Jacob's life. This last struggle came one quiet night as Jacob sat alone by a campfire on his journey back to his homeland. It was here that an angel of God came to wrestle with him.

The two wrestled until dawn. Only when the first light of day began to cast its shadow did the angel demand that Jacob let him go. The time had come to conclude their dramatic struggle and the other dramatic struggles of Jacob's life.

Jacob agreed to release the angel but on one condition: The man—this representative of God—must first pronounce a blessing on him.

> The man said, "Let me go, for it is daybreak."
>
> But Jacob replied, "I will not let you go unless you bless me."
>
> The man asked him, "What is your name?"
>
> "Jacob," he answered.
>
> Then the man said, "Your name will no longer be Jacob, but Israel, because you have struggled with God and with men and have overcome." (Gen. 32:26-28)

From the maturity of Jacob's faith and his deep appreciation of God's blessing, the nation of Israel received its name that night and moved momentously forward with God's enduring purpose.

Jacob's life of achievement and purpose can be your life, too, if you are willing to follow his example of growing faith and appreciation of God's blessing. After all, God's blessing is a central part of your birthright in Christ. When you accepted Jesus as your Savior, Father God blessed you "in the heavenly realms with every spiritual blessing in Christ" (Eph. 1:3). That's the incredible *berakhah* attached to the life of every Christian.

With your birthright blessing in Christ, you can expect genuine prosperity. You can expect God's help, favor, and daily support. And just like Jacob, you can expect to succeed no matter what challenge comes before you!

JOSHUA'S WORDS—THE DEVASTATION OF GOD'S CURSE

If Jacob was the one who understood the priceless value of God's blessing, then it was Joshua who grasped the devastating consequences of God's curse.

Joshua was Israel's leader after Moses died, and he led the people as they entered the Promised Land. One of the early outposts in this new land was the city of Jericho. When the Israelites approached that city, God told them to conquer and destroy it.

We know the story of how the army of Israel marched around the fortified walls of Jericho and how God caused those walls to fall. But there's more to the story of Jericho.

After the Israelites destroyed the city, God instructed Joshua to pronounce a curse over Jericho so no one would ever rebuild it without suffering great loss.

This was the curse Joshua pronounced over the city:

> At that time Joshua pronounced this solemn oath:
> "Cursed before the Lord is the man who undertakes
> to rebuild this city, Jericho:

"At the cost of his firstborn son will he lay its foundations; at the cost of his youngest will he set up its gates." (Josh. 6:26)

As time and generations passed, Joshua's curse over Jericho stood firm. Hundreds and hundreds of years swept by until one man finally decided to rebuild that city. His name was Hiel of Bethel.

When Hiel of Bethel began the rebuilding process, he lost his firstborn son. When he erected Jericho's gates, he lost his youngest. The events unfolded exactly as Joshua had pronounced them so many years before (1 Kings 16:34).

Do you see how lasting and powerful your faith-filled words can be? As Joshua revealed, our faith-filled words transcend the temporal world. They extend far beyond our limited definitions of time, space, and consequence. They are the life-changing and life-challenging words that can and will impact generations of men and women in the earth.

THE SONS OF THUNDER—BINDING AND LOOSING

In the Bible, the phrase "binding and loosing" is sometimes used to describe the pronouncement of God's blessing as well as his curse. Jesus used this phrase several times in the gospels when teaching his disciples about faith's commands.

"I tell you the truth, whatever you bind on earth will be bound in heaven, and whatever you loose on earth will be loosed in heaven," Jesus said to his disciples (Matt. 18:18).

Through example and practice, the disciples learned the lessons of binding and loosing well, perhaps none more than James and his brother John. First cousins of Jesus, through Mary's sister, Salome,

James and John were always at Jesus' side, eager to learn and advance themselves during the early days of their faith.

In the eyes of the other disciples, however, young James and John were more than just eager—they were bold, vocal, and brash. Remember, James and John were the two disciples who asked Jesus for honored seating in heaven; they wanted to sit at Jesus' right and left hand. They even recruited their mother to help press their request. Their boldness and tenacity created an uproar with Peter and the other disciples. (See Mark 10:35-45).

James and John were so bold, vocal, and brash in the early days of their ministry that Jesus gave them a special nickname. He called them "sons of thunder" (Mark 3:17).

My favorite sons of thunder story is recorded in Luke's gospel. It's here that we learn about a journey the two young men took to Jerusalem with Jesus and the other disciples. On this journey, their group was turned away by the citizens of a certain Samaritan village. The people of that village refused them both entry and passage.

The hostility of the Samaritans riled James and John immensely. With their emotions boiling, they said to Jesus, "Lord do you want us to call fire down from heaven to destroy them?" (Luke 9:54). James and John wanted to "fight fire with fire" quite literally.

On hearing their words, Jesus emphatically shook his head no. He then sat the two down to explain the immaturity of their thinking and the foolishness of their request.

So why do I enjoy this story so much? Isn't this a story that typifies rash thinking and immature judgment? Sure it does. But at the same time, it illustrates something bigger, brighter, and truly inspiring: It illustrates the strength and sincerity of two people's faith.

Do you see it? The sons of thunder were convinced they could call down fire from heaven just as Elijah had in generations past. There were no "ifs" or "maybes" to their faith. The only question was "Yes or no, Jesus?"—"Do you want us to call down fire or not, Jesus?"

Despite their immaturity, they were certain when it came to believing all that Jesus had taught them about faith's commands. With boldness and tenacity, young James and John grabbed hold of their empowerment and reveled in the magnitude of all they had been given.

ONE CLEAR VOICE FOR TODAY

Whenever I think about James and John and Christianity's authority to bind and loose, I imagine all that we as Christians could accomplish today if we came together as one united body. Imagine if together we began to pronounce God's blessings over our cities, towns, and communities? If we began to speak with one clear voice?

After all, we are called to be one body where the hands, feet, and individual parts function together in one accord. "The body is a unit, though it is made up of many parts; and though all its parts are many, they form one body. So it is with Christ" (1 Cor. 12:12).

In the book of Acts, the early believers showed us the miraculous accomplishments that can occur when Christians link their arms together. One central theme of this book is unity among God's men and women. It's a book that teaches us about "singleness of heart" and speaking in "one accord" (see Acts 1:14 and 2:46 KJV). It describes how a united Christian voice can shake the world around us.

"They lifted up their voice to God with one accord . . . and the place was shaken where they were assembled together" Paul tells us (Acts 4:24-31 KJV). By acting together, these early Christians shook the foundations of everything around them.

In the past, you and I have seen glimpses of how powerful and contagious this shaking can be when people come together with one voice. In my mind, I often go back to the days of the 1984 Detroit Tigers. With something as seemingly trivial as speaking "Bless you boys!" over a city and a sports team, the people of Detroit inspired a response and created an impact that altered lives and awakened communities. Those words—"Bless you boys!—became a powerful catalyst, a great wave, an unstoppable dynamic.

Think about the towering wave and the unstoppable dynamic we could create again if we began to speak blessings and encouragement over our homes, communities, cities, and countries. Think about the changes we would enjoy. Think about the benefits we all would experience.

We even know the exact catalyst to start the ball rolling in America: "God Bless America," the words of Irving Berlin's renowned song of faith. Just imagine the impact in the United States if Americans reclaimed the words of this special song.

Written almost one hundred years ago, this song once rang out across America's shores. Millions once celebrated these words of God's blessing:

> God bless America, land that I love.
> Stand beside her and guide her
> Through the night with the light from above.
>
> From the mountains, to the prairies
> To the oceans white with foam
> God bless America, my home sweet home.

It can happen again. I know it can. You know it can. We saw an early beginning in the days after 9/11 when Americans everywhere picked up these words of faith. We saw members of Congress from both parties come together on the Capitol steps to proclaim "God bless America!" We saw people grab hold of the words in their workplaces, community gatherings, and homes. Even Major League Baseball grabbed hold of the words for the crowds who filled their stadiums.

"God bless America, land that I love!"—remember how stirring it was to hear? It shocked the devil and his minions when America reached for these words during that time of tragedy. Throughout the dark days after 9/11, people knew these words of blessing needed to be said. From their hearts, the words rose up with meaning and had an impact. The words made a difference in America.

"God bless America, land that I love! God bless her . . . stand beside her . . . and guide her!"

It can happen again. We don't have to wait for tragedy or the pain of an economic downturn. We can begin today. From our hearts, we can pronounce God's blessings across our lands.

In every nation and country, the pronouncement of God's blessings sits waiting for willing voices. These words of faith call out to us all, every man and every woman. From these faith-filled words, God has promised to respond with his presence, countenance, help, and abundance.

It's time to start the ball rolling. With just three words uttered in faith, you and I can create a new avalanche that will bless all nations and peoples.

Personal Reflections

The words of God's blessings are the words of faith that belong to me. Through my pronouncement, God has agreed to enrich every life, family, and community.

By speaking the words of God's blessings, I can bring help and support to the world around me.

11

Giants, Rocks, and Other Life Lessons in Speaking

"If I have seen further, it is by standing on the shoulders of giants."

—Isaac Newton

"I have learned many of my greatest lessons through seeing the faith of Bible saints in action."

—Charles F. Stanley

There are many ways to learn lessons in life, some hard and some not so hard. The easiest and most efficient lessons are usually the ones we learn from others. By finding out what they did right and what they did wrong, we enjoy valuable, practical insights for our own journey—and avoid many pitfalls in the process.

In this chapter, let's explore three life lessons from those who went before us, lessons that will guide and inspire our words, commands, and pronouncements.

CONQUERING GIANTS—A LIFE LESSON FROM DAVID

One of the most dramatic examples of faith's commanding voice comes from the story of David's victory over Goliath. It's a story jam-packed with practical life lessons in speaking—yes, in speaking!

The events of David's conquest unfold in chapter 17 of 1 Samuel with the army of the Philistines assembled for battle against the army of Israel and Saul, Israel's King, leading his men.

In this battle, the Philistines had a special weapon: a man named Goliath, a true giant who stood over nine feet tall. Trained and honed for battle, he was a warrior's warrior, a complete fighting machine.

On his head, he wore a bronze helmet; over his chest, bronze armor; and tightened about his legs were thick bronze shielding. In the sunlight, his massive being glowed golden-red. He looked so ominous that everyone knew that hell itself had fashioned his adornments.

With a javelin strapped to his back and an enormous spear in his hand, Goliath would parade to the front line of battle each day, screaming for an Israelite to come forward to challenge him. For forty dreadful days, Goliath screamed and cursed at the men of Israel, demanding that someone step up to face him.

But no one would move. All of Israel, even King Saul, was terrified by the giant and his defiant words. The power of Goliath's words and the sight of his presence paralyzed every man.

After forty days of Goliath's torment, David—then just a teenage shepherd boy—came on the scene. He had come to the Israelite camp to deliver sheep and other supplies for the men. In God's timing, he arrived just as the soldiers were aligning for the day's confrontation.

David saw the soldiers take their places. He watched as Goliath paraded forward to begin his morning round of mayhem. He watched as the Israelite army froze in response.

David, however, didn't freeze. He wasn't terrified. David had faced menacing problems before and through his trust in God, David had overcome them all. David knew firsthand the power of his God in every battle and against every foe. Goliath, he knew, would be no different.

So with faith and courage rising up within him, David began to speak to the soldiers around him and even to King Saul. David told them he was more than able, through the power of God Almighty, the God of Israel, to slay the badgering Goliath. God, he told them, would stand with him and deliver Israel from the hands of the Philistines.

Look closely at the words David spoke to King Saul. These are the words of faith and conviction that moved a king to send a teenager, a mere shepherd boy, into combat against a champion warrior:

> But David said to Saul, "Your servant has been keeping his father's sheep. When a lion or a bear came and carried off a sheep from the flock, I went after it, struck it and rescued the sheep from its mouth. When it turned on me, I seized it by its hair, struck it and killed it.
>
> Your servant has killed both the lion and the bear; this uncircumcised Philistine will be like one of them because he has defied the armies of the living God. The Lord who delivered me from the paw of the lion and the paw of the bear will deliver me from the hand of this Philistine." (1 Sam. 17:34-37)

With Saul's consent, David strode forward to assault the Philistine strongman. And with every step, David kept speaking.

I can't overemphasize the words David spoke as he approached Goliath, for they resound in heaven even today. They are the words of faith's proclamation that pierced Goliath's bright bronze armor before David ever placed a single stone in his shepherd's sling.

Proclaimed David to Goliath:

> You come against me with sword and spear and javelin, but I come against you in the name of the Lord Almighty, the God of the armies of Israel, whom you have defied.
>
> This day the Lord will hand you over to me, and I'll strike you down and cut off your head. Today, I will give the carcasses of the Philistine army to the birds of the air and the beasts of the earth, and the whole world will know that there is a God in Israel.
>
> All those gathered here will know that it is not by sword or spear that the Lord saves; for the battle is the Lord's, and he will give all of you into our hands. (1 Sam. 17:45-47)

David's proclamation to Goliath wasn't "trash talking"—this was faith talking. David wasn't trying to "psych out" his opponent—he was speaking as a commander of God, a representative of God's heavenly forces.

"I come against you in the name of the Lord Almighty, the God of the armies of Israel" was how David put it to Goliath. His proclamation unmistakably identified the name—the ultimate source of the power, authority, and might—standing with him.

Beyond all doubt, David understood who he was and what kingdom he belonged to. He understood he was a member of God's kingdom and God's army. He understood his authority and commission and how his commanding words would be backed by God's own hand.

By faith, David knew the mountain of a man called Goliath would have to move aside once his faith-filled words were spoken.

Look what happened next. David followed up faith's words with faith's deeds: "David ran quickly toward the battle line" to attack Goliath and after reaching into his bag to remove a stone, David "slung it and struck the Philistine on the forehead" (1 Sam. 17:48-49).

The end result was faith's victory: "The stone sank into [Goliath's] forehead, and he fell face down on the ground." (1 Sam. 17:49).

The giant was dead. In panic and terror, the Philistine army fled the battlefield.

Through faith-filled words and faith-inspired deeds, David turned on the faucet of God's miraculous power. He put his faith into action; he gave a voice to his heart-held beliefs. The result was one of history's greatest conquests—one for everyone to see and for all generations to learn from.

The inspiring news is that David's success can be your success. Like David, we are empowered by God and Jesus Christ to command problems and obstacles—every menacing giant that taunts and confronts us—to move aside or suffer destruction. By faith, we can proclaim the end result of victory. By faith, we can win what appears to the outside world to be an impossible fight.

I don't know what Goliath you may be facing today. Maybe it's sickness. Maybe it's addiction. Maybe it's financial difficulties or some other turmoil. What I do know, however, is that you can boldly and confidently say to your problem, your Goliath:

> I come against you in the name of the Lord Almighty, the God of my kingdom and my army. This day the Lord has handed you over to me so I can cut off your head and strike you down.

> Today your carcass will be given to the birds of the air and the beasts of the earth, and the whole world will know there is a God in my home and community.

> The battle, power, and results are God's, and he has given you over to defeat this very day.

WATER FROM A ROCK—A LIFE LESSON FROM MOSES

Unlike David, Moses had an entirely different approach when it came to words: Avoid them whenever and wherever possible!

Of course, it's wasn't that Moses disliked words; rather words disliked him. You see, Moses had a serious speech impediment. In fact, words were so difficult for Moses that he begged and pleaded with God to send someone in his place to deliver Israel from slavery during the time of the Exodus.

"O Lord, I am not eloquent or a man of words," cried Moses, "for I am slow of speech, and have a heavy and awkward tongue" (Ex. 4:10 AMP).

"O Lord, please send someone else to do it," pled Moses (Ex. 4:13).

It was only as a consolation to Moses' many pleas that God finally agreed to send Aaron, Moses' brother, with him to act as Moses' mouthpiece. Aaron would be the skilled speaker Moses thought was necessary for God's mission to succeed. The agreement was this: Moses would tell Aaron exactly what to say, and Aaron in turn would speak the words before the Pharaoh of Egypt.

God also gave Moses a staff to help him announce and direct many of God's miracles. "Take this staff in your hand so you can perform miraculous signs with it," God instructed Moses (Ex. 4:17).

The Bible confirms how Moses used this staff to signal many of God's miracles during the time of the exodus from Egypt:

When Moses threw the staff on the ground, God transformed it into a snake. When Moses struck the waters of the Nile with it, God changed the water into blood. When Moses raised the staff, God raised up hordes of frogs and gnats to invade the land.

Moses' staff was a symbol of God's underlying power and strength. It was not a magic wand. Moses understood the distinction well. He knew faith was what bound him to God and what allowed their relationship to endure. Without this trust, Moses knew his staff had no value or meaning.

Over the course of his life, Moses grew to have one of the closest, most intimate and trusting relationships with God ever recorded in the Bible. With sincerity and in humbleness, he walked with the Lord and advanced heaven's goals on the earth. Moses was one of God's greatest heroes.

But even great and humble men of God have tests to endure and lessons to learn. For Moses, his difficult lesson occurred in the Desert of Zin at a place called Meribah Kadesh almost forty years after he triumphantly led his people out of Egypt.

It was at Meribah Kadesh that no water could be found for the people as they traveled toward the Promised Land. With their increasing thirst, complaints began to mount, and serious opposition gathered against Moses and Aaron. In response to the growing crisis, Moses sought the Lord's counsel.

The Lord was faithful, instructing Moses and Aaron as to what they should do. God told them to take the staff and assemble the Israelites. Once assembled, Moses was to speak to the special rock that had accompanied the Israelites on their long journey. Moses was to command this rock to pour forth water for the people to drink.

The Lord's instructions were very specific: Moses was not to strike the rock with his staff as he had in times past. No, this time, Moses was to speak to that rock and tell it to release its watery treasure:

> The Lord said to Moses, "Take the staff, and you and your brother Aaron gather the assembly together. Speak to that rock before their eyes and it will pour out its water. You will bring water out of the rock for the community so they and their livestock can drink." (Num. 20:7-8)

Moses followed the Lord's instruction as he gathered together the people of Israel. But Moses' willingness and trust in the Lord stopped here.

Instead of speaking to the rock, Moses rebuked the grumbling crowd and then took his staff and smashed it twice against the rock. Water gushed from the rock—but, unfortunately, so did the Lord's disappointment and anger.

The Bible describes the scene in the book of Numbers:

> Moses took the staff from the Lord's presence, just as he commanded him. He and Aaron gathered the assembly together in front of the rock and Moses said to them, "Listen, you rebels, must we bring you water out of this rock?"

Then Moses raised his arm and struck the rock twice with his staff. Water gushed out, and the community and their livestock drank.

But the Lord said to Moses and Aaron, "Because you did not trust in me enough to honor me as holy in the sight of the Israelites, you will not bring this community into the land I give them." (Num. 20:9-12)

We will never know why Moses refused to follow the Lord's instructions. God doesn't provide greater detail in the Bible.

Was it Moses' old nemesis, his difficulty with the spoken word, that had reared its ugly head? Was it frustration over God's timing of events for the traveling and complaining Israelites? Perhaps it was many factors.

And why didn't Aaron intervene?

Again, we don't know the details. And, quite frankly, it doesn't matter.

What we do know—and what matters—is that Moses and Aaron refused God by refusing to fully trust in him. After a lifetime of walking with God, God held them both to a higher standard of trust and obedience. When he asked them to open the faucet of his blessings by speaking faith's commands, he expected a loyal and faithful response.

In God's eyes, their mistrust was a refusal to honor him as holy before the assembled people of Israel. By not speaking faith's pronouncement to the rock at Kadesh, Moses and Aaron had refused to honor their faithful and loving friend—the same friend who had parted the Red Sea for them, who had humbled Pharaoh's armies, and who had lead their people out of slavery. The same friend who had sent manna from heaven and made sure that neither their sandals nor their clothing ever wore out. The same friend who had strengthened and physically sustained them in every miraculous way possible.

From this event at Meribah Kadesh, God's judgment fell on Moses and Aaron. Though both had reached the end of their natural lives, they would not be allowed to enter the Promised Land, which lay just steps ahead of them after their long journey. Sadly, they would end their earthly days on the other side of that special place, seeing it only from a distance.

The following passage from the book of Deuteronomy describes how Moses, then one hundred twenty years old, was permitted only to stand atop Mount Nebo in the Abarim range to look out on the glorious Promised Land that stretched before him.

As you read this passage, imagine the thoughts that raced through Moses' mind and the emotions of joy mixed with deep regret that consumed his heart:

> Then Moses climbed Mount Nebo from the plains of Moab to the top of Pisgah, across from Jericho. There the Lord showed him the whole land—from Gilead to Dan, all of Naphtali, the territory of Ephraim and Manasseh, all the land of Judah as far as the western sea, the Negev and the whole region from the Valley of Jericho, the City of Palms, as far as Zoar.
>
> Then the Lord said to him, "This is the land I promised on oath to Abraham, Isaac and Jacob when I said, 'I will give it to your descendants.' I have let you see it with your eyes, but you will not cross over into it."
>
> And Moses the servant of the Lord died there in Moab, as the Lord had said. He buried him in Moab,

in the valley opposite Beth Peor, but to this day no
one knows where his grave is. Moses was a hundred
and twenty years old when he died, yet his eyes were
not weak nor his strength gone. (Deut. 34:1-7)

The lesson of Moses and Aaron is difficult but one we each must
learn from. How many of us have missed our own promised land
by failing to speak faith's words to the problems and circumstances
in our lives? How many times have we refused to trust God by
remaining silent when we needed to speak? How often have our
mouths remained shut?

If we want to see the water of God's blessings released into our life
and community, we must be willing to open our mouth. It's through
both words and deeds that we put our faith into action. We must
honor both these ordained avenues of faith. Only by releasing God's
Word from our heart and mouth will we experience God's unlimited
power for change and success.

While we're reflecting here, let's not forget the work of the Holy
Spirit—the Spirit of truth, our counselor—whom God has so
graciously given us. The Holy Spirit is with us to lead and guide us
into truth.

In my own life's battles and throughout my ministry, the Holy Spirit
has led me to Scriptures that have fed my spirit. When I began to
release those truths from my mouth, the problems, obstacles, and
concerns facing me began to move aside. They had no choice.

At times, the Holy Spirit has even given me specific words to speak,
words consistent with God's Scriptures. Again, when I began to
speak these words, the changes necessary for my life began to unfold
around me. Until I spoke, however, nothing moved or changed.

What about you? Can you remember times in your own life when
the Holy Spirit has led you to Scriptures with the encouragement, if

not the urgency, to speak? Perhaps you remained silent because of concern over what others might think or say.

Take the lesson of Moses and Aaron to heart and begin speaking the words God has endeavored and encouraged us to proclaim. Open your big, bold, beautiful mouth to speak and release God's power into your life. Start today.

This same advice is for pastors, evangelists, and church leaders who have longed to see certain movements and demonstrations of God's power in their meetings and services. What has the Holy Spirit been tugging on your heart to speak? What messages from God's Word have you been reluctant to share despite God's encouragement?

The truth of God's Word spoken from our mouth is the mighty hammer, the consuming fire, and the nourishing grain for our life. As God tried to assure Moses from the very beginning, it's not the eloquence of our speech or the oratory skills of men and women that will move people's hearts and release God's supernatural power for change—it's our faith-filled words.

Rev. Billy Graham often emphasized this important point to us by saying, "I'm not a great man. I just have a great message."

Paul, in his letters to the churches, also stressed this point by saying:

> When I came to you, brothers, I did not come with eloquence or superior wisdom as I proclaimed to you the testimony about God. For I resolved to know nothing while I was with you except Jesus Christ and him crucified.
>
> My message and my preaching were not with wise and persuasive words, but with a demonstration of

the Spirit's power, so that your faith might not rest on
men's wisdom, but on God's power. (1 Cor. 2:1-5)

Isn't that the bottom line—speaking God's words and commands
from out of our earnest heart and willing mouth? By so doing, we
will release a demonstration of God's great power. By so doing, we
will see and experience the revolutionary changes and blessings we
each desire.

WHAT THEN SHALL WE SAY!—A LIFE LESSON FROM PAUL

In his writings, Paul opened up his life to us in vivid detail. He
didn't hide or sugarcoat any part of it. He laid it out for us, both the
ups and the downs. He gave us a truthful and candid look.

Paul shared his life because he wanted us to learn the lessons he had
learned by following Jesus Christ. He urged and prodded each of us
to study his words, examine his deeds, and scrutinize his life. To use
his life as our example for speaking, doing, and living.

"Whatever you have learned or received or heard from me, or seen
in me—put it into practice. And the God of peace will be with you,"
pled Paul (Phil. 4:9).

Over the course of my own life, I've taken Paul's urgings to heart.
Through the good and bad, the ups and downs, the successes
and failures, I've often looked to Paul's life for perspective and
wisdom.

Over and over, I've asked myself: How would Paul handle my
concern? What would he say here? What words, commands, and
pronouncements would he utter?

And countless times I've spoken the very words and commands
of faith that Paul himself first spoke so many centuries ago. I said

what he said. I acted as he acted. I put Paul's personal example into practice in my own life.

Perhaps it's only fitting then to conclude our chapter on life lessons by looking at a very special set of words Paul offered to all believers in his letter to the Roman church. It was in this letter, written more than two thousand years ago, that Paul thoroughly described our divine calling, celebrated standing, and supernatural empowerment as Christians. His letter stressed these honored and eternal aspects of our new life in Christ.

Paul then highlighted these great truths by offering words of faith to confront the problems and challenges we each must face on our earthly journey. In classic rhetorical fashion, this is what Paul shared with us:

> What, then, shall we say in response to this? If God
> is for us, who can be against us? (Rom. 8:31)

Bull's-eye. One all-encompassing acknowledgement for every challenge we may face: "If God is for us, who can be against us!" To every personal problem: "If God is for me, you can't be against me!" To every personal concern: "If God is for me, you can't overcome me!" To every mountain: "If God is for me, then you must move aside!" Clear. Arrestingly simple. Completely irrefutable.

When you know who you are as a Christian—your inheritance, position of authority, and empowerment in the kingdom of God and Christ— Paul's words become the words of your heart. When you know whom you trust, these words become the words you must speak. When you believe what the Father and the Son have told you about your new life, these words become your declaration, your proclamation, your battle cry.

God is for me, you can't be against me! God is for me, you can't defeat me! God is for me, you must move aside!

Keep these words close and ready at your side. Allow them to constantly echo in your heart as a reminder of what you have been given, what belongs to you.

Personal Reflections

By faith, I can proclaim the end result of victory in every battle and challenge.

By faith, I can release the water of God's blessings and provide a demonstration of his incomparable power.

By faith, I can speak the words and commands of someone who overcomes and enjoy God's complete success.

PART IV

THE GRATITUDE OF FAITH

THANKFUL EXPRESSION

12

Thanks and Praise: Speaking Faith's Most Rich and Rewarding Language

"Thanks—small word, big meaning."

—*Barbara Bartocci*

"When you praise God, you can't help but become a magnet that will attract all the blessings God has already prepared for your life!"

—*Bob Yandian*

In Washington, D.C., stands the Washington Monument, a stone obelisk that stands more than 555 feet tall. It's the tallest stone monument in the world and the tallest structure of any kind in the United States' capital.

Covered with the brightest white marble and jutting upward toward the stars, this remarkable monument is an expression of America's enduring gratitude to George Washington and all the founding fathers.

What few know, however, is that this monument pays tribute to one other special father. His name and the accompanying tribute appear at the very top on the east side capstone with the inscribed Latin words *Laus Deo.* The meaning of those words: "Praise be to God!"

Laus Deo is an expression of America's sincere gratitude to God our creator—the original founding father. Each morning as the sun's first rays light the capital of the United States, God sees those inscribed words and he smiles!

YOUR GRATITUDE BLESSES GOD

George Washington would be proud of the monument that bears his name, not because it thanks and honors him, but because it thanks and honors God Almighty, the one whose hand helped to join together Washington's great nation. During the many long and difficult days of the American Revolution, Washington knew God was with him and his fellow patriots. He recognized that God was intervening for their new country.

When victory in the fight for independence finally arrived, the American patriots understood how important it was to express their appreciation for God's help and favor. Expressing their gratitude was an indispensable step in their new beginning as a nation. So before the United States had even reached its first birthday, Washington, now president, proclaimed a special day of thanksgiving by announcing, "It is the duty of all nations to acknowledge the providence of Almighty God, to obey His will, to be grateful for His benefits, and humbly to implore His protection and favor."

From the opening pages of Genesis to the final chapter of Revelation, the message of gratitude to God is one that fills the Bible. Again and again, we are told that our words of thanks and praise bless God. These words hold exceptional value in his eyes.

In the book of Psalms, David focused closely on the blessing we offer God through our words of thanks and praise. He said, "I will bless the Lord at all times; his praise shall continually be in my mouth" (Ps. 34:1 KJV).

Pressing even further with his encouragement, David urged us to follow his example, saying, "O magnify the Lord with me, and let us exalt his name together" (Ps. 34:3 KJV).

Like David, all God's psalmists did an outstanding job sharing the message of thanks and praise. For them and all of Israel, the psalms represented a national treasure to guide them and inspire their gratitude for the Lord. Even to this day, Jews still traditionally refer to the book of Psalms by the Hebrew word *tehillim,* meaning "praises."

As a highlight to the many celebrated words of thanksgiving contained in that book, let's look at the opening verses of Psalm 103 where David shares with us with these timeless words of thanks and praise:

> Bless the Lord, O my soul; and all that is within me, bless his holy name.
>
> Bless the Lord, O my soul, and forget not all his benefits; who forgiveth all thine iniquities; who healeth all thy diseases;
>
> Who redeemeth thy life from destruction; who crowneth thee with lovingkindness and tender mercies;
>
> Who satisfieth thy mouth with good things; so that thy youth is renewed like the eagle's. (Ps. 103:1-5 KJV)

The Amplified Bible adds further emphasis to David's words by clarifying the use of the word "bless" to mean our "affectionate, grateful praise":

> Bless—affectionately, gratefully praise—the Lord, O
> my soul, and all that is [deepest] within me, bless His
> holy name!
>
> Bless—affectionately, gratefully praise—the Lord, my
> soul, and forget not [one of] all His benefits. (Ps. 103:1-
> 2 AMP)

How utterly astounding! Our affectionate, grateful praise blesses
God! Think about that. My words and your words of thanksgiving
generously give back to our creator. They surround, move, and
delight him. The Bible says God inhabits or lives within them: "O
thou that inhabitest [our] praises" (Ps. 22:3 KJV).

Your Gratitude Expresses Your Trust

In this book, we've learned about faith-filled words and their
importance in our lives. But our study of these unique and distinctive
words would not be complete without understanding that our words
of thanks and praise also express our faith in God.

Yes, the words of thanks and praise are, most definitely, faith-filled.
They capture and express the full measure of our trust in God.

To understand this point, consider what your words of thanks and
praise say or convey about you. Think about the personal meaning
behind these words. Think about the intention.

With your words of thanks and praise, are you saying you trust
God? Are you declaring him to be your rock, your champion? Do
your words of praise demonstrate your confidence in him?

The answers to these questions reveal the heart of faith that speaks
so clearly through words of thanks and praise. With our words of
gratitude, we loudly express our trust in God. We express our belief

in his power, wisdom, and goodness. With our words of thanks and praise, we declare to God—and the entire world around us—that we have full confidence and assurance in him and his promises.

For believers, this is rich language. Using these special words, I can express my faith generously. I can express my trust completely. With these words, I can boldly acknowledge the God and the Savior I hold so dear.

Let me offer another example to help underscore this voice of faith that speaks so effectively through our words of thanks and praise. The example again comes from David, now King David. Listen to King David's words here; listen to the expression of his heart:

> David blessed the Lord before all the assembly, and said, "Be praised, adored and thanked, O Lord, the God of Israel our [forefather], forever and ever.
>
> "Yours, O Lord, is the greatness, and the power, and the glory, and the victory, and the majesty; for all that is in the heavens and the earth is Yours; Yours is the kingdom, O Lord, and Yours it is to be exalted as head over all.
>
> "Both riches and honor come from You, and You reign over all. In Your hand are power and might; in Your hand it is to make great and to give strength to all.
>
> "Now therefore, our God, we thank You and praise Your glorious name and those attributes which that name denotes. (1 Chron. 29:10-13 AMP)

In every verse, David offers up his unshakeable trust in the Lord. With every word, he shows us his faith. David's words undeniably demonstrate that personal relationship of trust that defines faith at its deepest and most meaningful level.

In David's verses, we also see the sincerity of his heart. His words don't patronize or pretend; his words don't bluff or embellish. His words express honest and heartfelt sincerity that pleases God.

"I will praise you, O Lord, with all my heart," explains the psalmist (Ps. 9:1). That's what matters most to God. From your grateful heart and my grateful heart come faith's most moving expressions. Lip service, no matter how fancy or eloquent, will never make the grade.

"Sing and make music in your heart to the Lord, always giving thanks to God the Father for everything, in the name of our Lord Jesus Christ," guides Paul (Eph. 5:19-20). The grateful words and melodies of our heart move our heavenly father. This is the expression that blesses him and puts our faith into vibrant motion.

As soon as God hears these magnificent words of our heart, he instantly responds by throwing open the doors of his throne room, ushering us close for fellowship, counsel, and attention.

> On your feet now—applaud God! Bring a gift of laughter, sing yourselves into his presence.
>
> Enter with the password: "Thank you!" Make yourselves at home, talking praise. Thank him. Worship him.
>
> For God is sheer beauty, all-generous in love, loyal always and ever. (Ps. 100:1-2, 4-5 MSG)

"I BELIEVE, THEREFORE I GIVE THANKS AND PRAISE"

When we offer God our thanks and praise, aren't we also following that important blueprint of faith that's been stressed repeatedly throughout this book? "I believe, therefore I speak"—our model of faith in action.

Do you recognize the pattern here? Faith means trusting God. Faith also means believing God's promises that have been recorded for our benefit. If this is what we genuinely hold in our heart—what we trust and believe—then from our heart must surely come the words of thanks and praise. So A leads and inspires us to express B.

Another helpful way to describe this inward-to-outward show of faith is to say that because we trust God and believe his promises, we respond by expressing the gratitude God deserves in return. Put in the most personal terms: "I believe who God is in my life and the great blessings he has promised me, therefore I give him my thanks and praise."

Let me share one last example to cement our understanding of faith's outward expression through our words of thanksgiving. The example comes from the life of Abraham and involves God's promise that Abraham would have a child and ultimately become "the father of many nations" (Gen. 15:4-5, 17:4; Rom. 4:17).

Abraham trusted God completely, and he believed God's promise of a child who would carry on his legacy. For Abraham, this was the truth for his life. Despite his old age and his barren wife, Sarah, Abraham was "fully persuaded that God had power to do what he had promised" (Rom. 4:21).

So while the world laughed at Abraham and Sarah, Abraham did something grand and faith filled: He gave thanks and praise to God. Because he trusted God and believed God's promise of a child, Abraham responded with thanks and praise to his promise keeper.

> He did not waiver through unbelief regarding the promise of God, but was strengthened in his faith and gave glory to God, being fully persuaded that God had power to do what he had promised. (Rom. 4:20-21)

Do you recognize how thanks and praise was the outward expression of Abraham's faith? The rich language of Abraham's inward trust? By giving glory to God, Abraham voiced his unwavering confidence in all that God had promised him.

Thanks and praise are the words of faith. They have faith stuffed into every letter and every syllable. And just like the other faith-filled words we've studied in earlier chapters, these words represent the same bold expression that places God's hand in the middle of our circumstances.

If you're looking for a proven way to open the faucet of God's power and blessings for your life, grab hold of the words of thanks and praise. If you're looking to turbo-charge your voice of faith, add words of thanks and praise. If you're searching for just the right faith-filled words to speak into your life and concerns, use the words of gratitude. You'll find no more perfect words to speak.

Your Gratitude Keeps You Rooted in Faith

We live in a unique age. We certainly could call it "the age of impatience"— the age when even instant gratification isn't quick enough.

Today it's all about fast and faster: Internet speeds, sound bites, fast foods, immediate profits. Get it sooner; grow it quicker; make it faster!

Today, as long as it's lightning fast, it's good. If it's gradual, reflective, or requires any nurturing, forget it. There's simply no time to lose.

Unfortunately, God doesn't operate on our timetable. He has his own perfect timetable for everything. In God's world, the words that carry the greatest weight are *patience* and *persistence*. Growth, maturity, and lasting success in his world always come with these qualities.

As we walk in faith with God, he guides and encourages each of us to become men and women of patience and persistence, people who refuse to give up our trust regardless of how long it takes for the final results to appear. He wants us to trust his timing for everything, no matter how fast or slow that timing may seem to the world around us.

"Imitate those who through faith and patience inherent what has been promised," counsels Heb. 6:12.

The Bible sometimes compares faith's patience to that of a farmer. "See how the farmer waits for the land to yield its valuable crop and how patient he is for the autumn and spring rains. You too, be patient and stand firm" (James 5:7-8).

Like that wise and patient farmer, we are to stand firm with the confidence that our valuable crop of end results will arrive at the right time in the correct season.

Consider also the example of Abraham. Abraham waited in faith for more than twenty-five years before God's promise of a child came to be. At the time of Isaac's birth, Abraham was almost one hundred years old. That's a lot of patience, yet it was God's perfect timing for Isaac's arrival.

Of course, we know Abraham had a proven approach, which he followed to help him stay rooted in faith during those years of waiting. What was this approach? What allowed him to keep his faith so strong and alive? Abraham thanked and praised God! That's how he stayed rooted. That's how he kept his eyes and his trust fastened on God Almighty, his promise keeper.

In our walk of faith, I can't overemphasize the importance of thanks and praise. Thanks and praise takes our eyes off the problem, a timetable, and all other influences that seek to steal and hinder our faith. Thanksgiving allows us to rise up above it all—above fear, doubt, a timeline, an earthly perspective.

From the higher perspective of thanksgiving, we see past the storms, the mountains, and our problems. From this higher perspective, all that comes into our view is an eternal loving Father and a victorious Savior. We see their hands stretched before us. Even more, we see the end result of success and victory set in place for us, fully accomplished by them.

Follow the wisdom of Abraham by allowing the words of thanks and praise to be the companion of your trust. Whenever you feel anxious, concerned, or frustrated about the timing of God's results in your life, reach for words of thanks and praise. Allow those words to encourage your heart and support all you do as you wait patiently for the success and victory God has for you.

"You know your way around faith. Now do what you've been taught. School's out; quit studying the subject and start living it! And let your living spill over into thanksgiving!" (Col. 2:7 MSG).

YOUR GRATITUDE BRINGS BLESSINGS

Let me share with you one more invaluable truth about your thanks and praise before God: Your gratitude brings increased blessings for your life.

If you reflect on my statement for even a moment, isn't it irrefutable? When we bless God with our heartfelt thanks and praise, how can he do anything but respond to us with blessings in return? After all, that's his nature, desire, and purpose for each of us. He wants to bless us, and when he's done blessing us, he wants to bless us even more.

Look at how the psalmist describes this truth in Ps. 89:15. He says before God, "Blessed are those who have learned to acclaim you." That's heaven's promise for you and me. When we thank God, he blesses us. When we praise God, he blesses us. He responds to our heart with his own heart.

In Psalm 67, the psalmist again confirms this great truth for us by saying: "May the peoples praise you, O God; may all the peoples praise you. Then the land will yield its harvest, and God, our God, will bless us" (Ps. 67:5-6).

I enjoy how Bob Yandian, a pastor and gifted Bible teacher, wonderfully put this proposition: "When you praise God, you can't help but become a magnet that will attract all the blessings God has already prepared for your life!"

A thankful heart and an open mouth make you a magnet for God's blessings. The gratitude of faith opens wide the faucet of his benefits. Embrace this most-basic truth and your life will change, forever.

Your Gratitude—It's the Right Thing

Expressing our faith and becoming a magnet for God's blessings are certainly inspiring reasons for offering up our thanksgiving, but there's an even more fundamental reason you and I should give thanks and praise to God: It's the right thing to do!

Think about it. In our daily lives, we give thanks and praise to those who help, support, and guide us. We give thanks and praise to those who bless us. We share our gratitude with those who share their efforts and talents with us. How much more then should we give thanks and praise to God, the one who daily provides for us? How much more for Jesus Christ—God the Son—who died for us?

In our hearts, we know it's fitting to give thanks. Deep down, we realize we each owe a debt of gratitude to God. Yet how often do we forget to repay it? With all the activities of our busy lives, how many times have we overlooked it? I know I have.

In the story of the ten lepers from Luke's gospel, Jesus reminded us how important it is to repay our debt of gratitude. In that story, ten lepers were miraculously healed by the power of God, but only one (a Samaritan) returned to give thanks and praise.

"One of them, when he saw he was healed, came back, praising God in a loud voice. He threw himself at Jesus' feet and thanked him" (Luke 17:15-16).

Jesus said to this man, "Were not all ten cleansed? Where are the other nine? Was no one found to return and give praise to God except this foreigner?" (Luke 17:17-18).

Look again at Jesus' words here: "Were not all ten cleansed? Where are the other nine?" His words represent great wisdom for our life, wisdom we can't dismiss or ignore. Wisdom we must put into action.

Whenever I reflect on the story of the ten lepers, I think back to what Sparky Anderson, the Detroit Tigers' baseball manager, did when his team won the final game of the 1984 World Series during that special season of dreams. When the final pitch was thrown, the final out called, and as the hometown crowd screamed in wild celebration, Anderson's first reaction was something you probably wouldn't expect from a weathered and crusty baseball manager.

What did he do? "First, I thanked God," said Anderson in his book *Bless You Boys: Diary of the Detroit Tigers' 1984 Season*. Before he did or said anything else, Anderson expressed his gratitude to God for the great victory and the other blessings in his life.

After he thanked God, Anderson thanked and praised every one of his players. He was grateful for all they had contributed to make the season a success. Only then, after he had paid his debt of gratitude, did Anderson join in Detroit's celebration for one of the most remarkable teams and seasons in Major League Baseball history.

Anderson was a very wise man.

Personal Reflections

When I give thanks and praise to God, I bless him. I give back to him in a most important and valuable way.

When I give thanks and praise to God, I express my trust in him and my belief in his promises.

Thanks and praise is the language of faith that opens wide the faucet of God's blessings for my life.

13

Counting Your Blessings

"Plenty of people miss their share of happiness, not because they never found it, but because they didn't stop to enjoy it."

—*William Feather*

"He is a wise man who does not grieve for the things which he has not but rejoices for those which he has."

—*Epictetus*

"I'm so thankful. I'm so blessed," said the old man as he sat on the bench, tying the laces on his running shoes and making sure the support and fit was just right. "To be able to run and exercise my body is something I'm so fortunate to do," he added, looking in my direction.

He could tell I didn't share his enthusiasm about our upcoming workouts at the local health club. Maybe it was my muttering about the drudgery of another day's exercise that tipped him off. Or maybe it was just the apathetic look plastered so generously across my face. Whatever it was, I knew that he knew I wasn't the least bit thankful about another day at the gym.

Trying to be polite, I mumbled a barely recognizable "Yes, you're right" before slamming my locker and shuffling out the door.

But he was right. I had the wrong attitude, the wrong perspective, the wrong mindset.

As I stepped on the treadmill and listened to the machine begin its familiar wind and grind, I thought more about what the man had said. I was fortunate to be running, moving my arms and legs, exercising my body. What an incredible gift to be breathing deeply, working my muscles, and taking in the sights and sounds around me. What a blessing! Such great fortune! I was indeed a very blessed man.

We have so much to be thankful for, don't we? To be alive. To enjoy the beauty of the earth and the wonders of the sky. To walk, talk, hear, and see all that surrounds us. To live in a time of great technology and change. To enjoy the personal comforts and medical advancements this age has brought us.

It's incredible. This grand adventure of life—our grand adventure—is something so fantastic and amazing.

But sadly, how often do we really appreciate our daily lives? We overlook so much of it, don't we? We take things for granted. We gloss over. We rarely stop to value all we have, all God has given us.

Instead of valuing what we have, our usual approach is to focus on what we don't have. We talk and complain about how life would be so much better "if only." If only we had this. If only we could do that. If only. If only. A tireless game of excuses, qualifiers, and psychological delays that rolls on and on.

In the meantime, the blessings and the wonders of God and life slip right past us. They become invisible to us.

Only when we've lost someone or something do most of us stop to appreciate the great value of what we had. Only when it's gone do we see the blessings that once stood before us. Only then, when it's too late, do we grasp the beauty, treasure, and magnificence of the people, events, and qualities that have graced our lives.

So how do we change? How do we break this pattern, this cycle, this negative approach to life?

The secret is found in the old man's words to me: Be thankful! Live an appreciative life! Each day, approach your life with an attitude of gratefulness and a mouth filled with thanksgiving.

With a grateful heart and an open mouth, we can revolutionize our existence. Gratitude will brighten our days and cause a richness of life to reemerge and overtake us. With thanksgiving, we will find a new energy and a renewed vitality for each and every day. In turn, all the blessings and wonders of life will suddenly become visible to us once again.

God shared with us this secret to living when he said, "In everything give thanks; for this is the will of God in Christ Jesus concerning you" (1 Thess. 5:18 KJV).

The Amplified Bible says it like this: "Thank [God] in everything— no matter what the circumstances may be, be thankful and give thanks; for this is the will of God for you [who are] in Christ Jesus" (1 Thess. 5:18 AMP).

In everything, give thanks. Each day, at every opportunity, look around and appreciate all that God has done for you. Value everything. See and smell every rose. And then express your thanks and praise to him.

COUNTING AND THEN EXPRESSING EVERY BENEFIT

God had David and the psalmists share this message of an appreciative life in many of their psalms. Look again at the wisdom shared with us in Psalm 103:

> Bless the Lord, O my soul; and all that is within me, bless his holy name.
>
> Bless the Lord, O my soul, and forget not all his benefits; who forgiveth all thine iniquities; who healeth all thy diseases;
>
> Who redeemeth thy life from destruction; who crowneth thee with lovingkindness and tender mercies;
>
> Who satisfieth thy mouth with good things; so that thy youth is renewed like the eagle's. (Ps. 103:1-5 KJV)

God's wisdom and instructions for living are concrete: We must count our blessings. Count, consider, and reflect on every good and beneficial aspect of your life. Remember and value what God has done for you in the past and what he is doing for you now. "Forget not all his benefits"—not even one.

Once we've counted, God then asks us to open our mouth to express our thanks and praise before him. An appreciative life is one built around a grateful heart and a big, bold, expressive mouth. Express your gratitude. Speak it! Say it! Thank God for all your blessings.

"Blessed be the Lord, who daily loadeth us with benefits, even the God of our salvation," declared David each day of his life (Ps. 68:19 KJV). He counted every blessing and then he blessed God with his words of gratitude.

How to Make Thanksgiving Your Daily Habit

To live an appreciative life, God gave us one other important instruction: Make it a daily habit.

David put it like this: "I will bless the Lord at all times; his praise shall continually be in my mouth" (Ps. 34:1 KJV).

To build a life of thanksgiving, David had to make giving thanks part of his daily routine. He couldn't give thanks once in a while or on special occasions. Only an everyday practice would bring the revolutionary results he desired for his life.

David and his fellow psalmists called this daily routine of thanksgiving a good habit. "It is good to praise the Lord and make music to your name, O Most High, to proclaim your love in the morning and your faithfulness at night" (Ps. 92:1-3).

But how do we create this good habit? The easy answer, of course, is just do it. Every day, give thanks and praise to God. Every day, express your gratitude. Practice until thanksgiving becomes habitual.

But I know getting started is often the most difficult part of a practice such as this. So to help get you started, here are five exercises to jump-start your habit of thanksgiving:

No. 1: Your Personal Book of Gratitude

On a sheet of paper, in a notebook, or, for those who are digitally inclined, on your smartphone, start a personal book of gratitude to record your blessings. Every day, write down one thing that you are thankful for. It can be anything: an event, a person, a smile, a word of encouragement, a parking space. Big or small, write it down. By recording that one thing, you will begin a daily routine.

Also, each month, write down one promise from God's Word that you are thankful for. As you record this promise in your book of gratitude, stop to consider how important it is for your life and family. Examine God's promise from every angle.

Then, each day, in your own words, give thanks to God for that one blessing and that one promise.

This simple "one blessing, one promise" exercise will build a productive habit into your life. It will develop a habit that governs your day and guides your week.

No. 2: Add Thanksgiving to Every Prayer

Every time you pray, make it an opportunity to give thanks and praise to God. We're good at making requests to God, but here's our opportunity to become equally good at giving thanks to him for his goodness and faithfulness.

Paul advocated this approach to prayer when he said, "Devote yourselves to prayer, being watchful and thankful" (Col. 4:2).

Paul also practiced what he preached. In every prayer he prayed for believers in the New Testament, Paul included his personal thanks and praise to God. He never missed this perfect opportunity to offer up his gratitude.

"We always thank God, the father of our Lord Jesus Christ, when we pray for you," said Paul in Col. 1:3. He understood the benefits.

No. 3: Start a Special Thankfulness Project

With a group of friends, consider writing down the Scriptures that tell you who you are in Christ. In the Bible, primarily the New

Testament, there are 140 verses that detail who you are and what you've been given through your faith in Jesus Christ. These verses belong to you.

When we focus our thoughts on what these Scriptures tell us about our new life in Christ, we can't help but give thanks and praise to God and Jesus. Our gifts and blessings in Christ will always inspire sincere thankfulness in us.

Paul shared this wisdom and practice with us when he wrote, "Have the roots [of your being] firmly and deeply planted [in Christ]—fixed and founded in Him—being continually built up in Him, becoming increasingly more confirmed and established in the faith, just as you were taught, and abounding and overflowing in it with thanksgiving" (Col. 2:7 AMP).

No. 4: Become Active in Your Church

In your church, take an active part in the praise and worship service. Sing and express your thanks. Don't sit back—get vocal. Add both your heart and your mouth to the gratitude your congregation gives to God and Jesus Christ.

I can't stress this enough: Go to church, get active in your congregation, and get involved with your group's expression of thanks and praise. This is your ideal opportunity to build a life of gratitude and appreciation that will transform all you do.

No. 5: Wear the Glasses of Gratitude

The "rose-colored glasses" God asks us to wear each day are the glasses of gratitude. He wants us to continually see our life and circumstances through the eyes of thankfulness. He wants us to appreciate the countless wonders around us and the countless miracles he performs for us daily. He wants us to observe, grasp, and cherish everything—and give thanks to him.

Now I know what you're thinking: "But what about my problems, struggles, and concerns? God's not asking me to give thanks for these, is he?"

Let's look again at God's instructions in 1 Thessalonians: "Thank [God] in everything—no matter what the circumstances may be, be thankful and give thanks; for this is the will of God for you" (1 Thess. 5:18 AMP).

Do you see the answer? God's not asking us to thank the problem; he's asking us to thank him. When we're in the middle of our tests, trials, and battles, he's asking us to lift up our voice to him because he's on our side and working for our benefit. In the middle of our greatest battle, God is there with us, ensuring victory in the end.

Look also at the King James translation of 1 Thess. 5:18, which emphasizes "in everything give thanks." "In" is the operative word here. In the middle of whatever you are going through, give thanks to God. No matter how bad or how hard the circumstances, give thanks to God. He knows the beginning from the end. He has a plan and your answer. He holds your blessing.

ONE STEP BACK IS OFTEN MANY LEAPS FORWARD

God knows the beginning from the end. He has a special plan for each of us that holds great blessings. You and I may not see them at first, but that's no reason to withhold our thanks.

At first, I'm sure Joseph didn't see God's great plan as he sat in a pit while his brothers debated whether to kill him or sell him into slavery. When the desert tribe of slave traders bound young Joseph, then seventeen, and carried him off to a foreign land to sell as a servant, I'm sure Joseph still didn't see an inspired plan or godly blessing in this.

Eventually, though, Joseph began to understand God had a plan and a bigger purpose in the tragedy unfolding around him. As Joseph continued to trust and give thanks to God, he began to see that God's hand was in everything. He began to recognize that God was with him, even in the dark pit. He realized that God was working out a special blessing and a greater purpose in all these adversities.

Others saw it as well. Potiphar, the wealthy Egyptian nobleman, saw God's hand in Joseph's life and because of it, he put Joseph in charge of everything he owned.

"[Potiphar] his master saw that the Lord was with [Joseph] and how the Lord caused all that he did to prosper in [Joseph's] hand. So Joseph found favor in his sight, and became his personal servant; and he made him overseer over his house, and all that he owned he put in his charge" (Gen. 39:3-4 NASB).

The Pharaoh of Egypt saw God's hand in Joseph's life just as clearly and because of it, he put Joseph, now thirty, in charge of all of Egypt.

"Since God has made all this known to you," said the Pharaoh, "there is no one so discerning and wise as you. You shall be in charge of my palace, and all my people are to submit to your orders. Only with respect to the throne will I be greater than you" (Gen. 41:39-40).

When famine came over the entire region and as Joseph's brothers traveled to Egypt in search of food and survival, Joseph, now head of Egypt, knew it was time to reveal God's great plan and purpose even to them.

He told his frightened brothers: "Don't be afraid. Am I in the place of God? You intended to harm me, but God intended it for good to accomplish what is now being done, the saving of many lives" (Gen. 50:19-20).

Joseph further confirmed to his brothers, "And now, do not be distressed and do not be angry with yourselves for selling me here, because it was to save lives that God sent me ahead of you" (Gen. 45:5).

Over the course of thirteen years, God's plan for Joseph's life came to fruition. God knew the beginning from the end. What seemed like only tragedy, distress, and intense struggle was actually a divine plan and a grand blessing for Joseph and thousands of other people.

God knows the beginning from the end in your life, too. What at first may seem like only adversity and struggle may very well be God positioning and moving you forward to higher heights, bigger blessings, and greater good. By trusting him and remaining thankful in the middle of it all, you will see God's plan come to fruition.

"For I know the plans I have for you," declares the Lord, "plans to prosper you and not to harm you, plans to give you hope and a future" (Jer. 29:11).

Stay focused on the one who holds the plan and the purpose for your life. Give him continual thanks and praise during every challenge and every struggle. In the end, you will enjoy success and countless other blessings.

STORMS—THE PRICELESS PROVING OF YOUR FAITH

The challenges and struggles of life offer another important and beneficial opportunity for us. Martin Luther King Jr. addressed this opportunity when he said, "The ultimate measure of a man is not where he stands in moments of comfort but where he stands at times of challenge and controversy."

Martin Luther King certainly understood times of challenge and controversy. He understood those are candid times in a person's life—times that transcend pretense, times that reveal so much about us on the inside. Only in these times of adversity, King felt, could a man or a woman fully learn what he or she was capable of standing for, fighting for, and ardently achieving.

Consider King's words from the perspective of your own life. Have you ever boasted about an inner strength or personal conviction only to find out you didn't fully measure up to your own expectations once confronted or challenged by others? Or, the opposite, have you ever lamented about a perceived weakness in your life only to later realize you had misjudged your own capabilities and convictions?

Or, to push the introspection even further, have you ever mistakenly (or perhaps knowingly) put on a false front about some aspect of your life?

I have to answer yes to all the above. You probably do too. Misjudging, mistaking, and even pretending to be someone or something we're not are errors everyone makes at some point. It's all part of being human.

But what happens when the storms hit? When the times of challenge and adversity come to confront us (and they will), our false assumptions get blown away. Bluffing can't resist a storm; pretense can't withstand its fury. In the storms of life, all we have and all that remains is what's genuine.

Sometimes, unfortunately, we find out we didn't have what we thought we had. We come up short. More often, however, we find out that we had more inside us than we ever assumed or imagined. Because of the storm, we uncover great strengths, genuine courage, and other hidden qualities that we're living inside us.

Storms work the same way in our faith life. We can claim and assert and put on a convincing face about our trust in God, but when the storms of life hit, we find out whether our faith is genuine. Do I really trust God? Do I really believe his promises? Where do I stand?

Sometimes we find out we didn't have the faith we thought we had. We come up short. Most often, however, we learn something remarkable about ourselves: that we had more faith, more fight, more courage and trust in our heart than we ever thought, assumed, or imagined. The storm proved out what we couldn't otherwise see, measure, or experience in the "good times."

Just as remarkable, in the storm, we prove that our God is everything we trusted and believed he would be—and more. We learn, firsthand, that our God is a God of his word. A God who promises that he will never leave us or forsake us and is true to that promise. A God who promises that he will carry us through every challenge and problem, and does.

Perhaps no one said it better than Peter when he described the great value and personal gain we receive by the proving of our faith in the tests and trials of life:

> Though now for a little while you may have had to suffer grief in all kinds of trials. These have come so that your faith—of greater worth than gold, which perishes even though refined by fire—may be proved genuine and may result in praise, glory and honor when Jesus Christ is revealed. (1 Peter 1:6-7)

Genuine faith—faith that's been tried, tested, and proven true in your life—is what comes out of the storms of life. This storm-tested, battle-proven faith is more precious than gold.

When we look at life's challenges from this broader perspective, our struggles take on a deeper meaning, don't they? Sure, these challenges are still difficult. Sure, these adversities are still painful. No one wants difficulty in his or her life. But they offer us the unmatched opportunity to prove for ourselves that God is faithful and his Word, which we have in our heart, is genuine and true.

Through the storms of life, we gain what no one can ever take away from us. That's priceless value. That's a blessing to be counted and something to rejoice and give thanks to God about.

YOUR OPPORTUNITY TO REASSESS, RECOMMIT, AND GROW

The final benefit that comes from life's challenges and adversities is the opportunity to reassess and recommit our lives. The storms of life force us to stop, look, and reexamine everything. They force us to ask ourselves the hard questions and to make important decisions.

In a magazine interview, actor Leonardo DiCaprio described the process of personal reassessment perfectly: "I've seen people have near-death experiences or lose things that are really important to them, then they stop and say, 'What is this junk that I'm focusing on? Why can't I just be happy to put my pants on in the morning?'"

What is the junk we're focused on? Why can't we just be happy putting our pants on in the morning? In the storms of life, we are forced to ask ourselves these critical questions and answer them honestly. These are the questions and the answers that bring us the opportunity for lasting change.

In a June 2005 commencement address to the Stanford University graduating class, Steve Jobs, founder of Apple Inc., spoke about some of the difficult times in his own life and how those storms forced him to ask and answer many life-defining questions.

In his speech, Jobs talked about how in 1985, at the age of thirty, he was fired from Apple, the company he had started in his parents' garage with partner Steve Wozniak.

Jobs explained that he had been fired from the company he had grown into a two billion dollar enterprise with more than four thousand employees. Equally as upsetting, he explained that he had been fired by an executive whom he had hired to help manage the company. Jobs' own man had pushed him out the door.

In his address, Jobs was candid about his embarrassment and pain. He told the young men and women of Stanford how the firing devastated him and how he felt he had let down a generation of entrepreneurs:

> So at thirty, I was out—and very publicly out. What had been the focus of my entire adult life was gone, and it was devastating.
>
> I really didn't know what to do for months. I felt that I had let the previous generation of entrepreneurs down—that I had dropped the baton as it was being passed to me.

He openly told the Stanford graduates, "I was a very public failure, and I even thought about running away from the valley."

After his firing and as the days passed, however, something extraordinary began to happen: Jobs took a closer look at his life and his path. He reassessed his goals, passions, and dreams. What he realized was that he still had a great love for creating new products and technologies.

"Something slowly began to dawn on me—I still loved what I did," recounted Jobs.

And with that, Jobs made a decision to recommit and start over.

Over the next several years, he started a company called NeXT and another company called Pixar. Through Pixar, Jobs brought groundbreaking technology to animated filmmaking, producing the world's first computer-animated feature film, *Toy Story*. That was followed by hit after hit, including movies such as *Finding Nemo* and *A Bug's Life*. The explosive success of Pixar eventually led to a decision by the Walt Disney Company to acquire Pixar, making Jobs a majority shareholder of Disney.

But that's only part of Jobs' comeback story. Eyeing the innovative computer technologies developed by Jobs at NeXT, the executives at Apple decided to purchase that company. It was this acquisition that brought Jobs back to Apple, the company he had started so many years before.

On his return, Jobs began a new era at Apple, leading, guiding, and reinventing the company to become a 21st century titan with such cutting-edge products as the iPod, iPhone, and iPad. From music to telecommunications to computers, Apple, under Jobs, brought fresh ideas and a creative vision that transformed these lucrative global industries.

With its resurgence, Apple became one of the most valued and respected companies on the planet. And Jobs became one of the most admired and acclaimed entrepreneurs of modern time.

Retelling the amazing story of his comeback and success, Jobs emphasized to the Stanford class how his firing from Apple played a pivotal role:

> I didn't see it then, but it turned out that getting fired from Apple was the best thing that could have ever happened to me. The heaviness of being successful was replaced by the lightness of being a beginner

again, less sure of everything. It freed me to enter one
of the most creative periods of my life.

Jobs also told them, "I'm pretty sure none of this would have
happened if I hadn't been fired from Apple. It was awful-tasting
medicine, but I guess the patient needed it."

The storms, challenges, and adversities of life affect everyone. We
can't avoid them. But as awful tasting as that medicine is, these are
the times that give us exceptional opportunities to grow.

So stay thankful. Lead an appreciative life! And most importantly,
"In everything give thanks; for this is the will of God in Christ Jesus
concerning you" (1 Thess. 5:18 KJV).

Personal Reflections

I'm so thankful. I'm so blessed. My life is the great gift God has given to me.

I give thanks and praise to God in every situation and circumstance because I know that he has a plan for my life, one that will bless, benefit, and prosper me and many others.

14

Choosing to Be Who You Already Are

"A rose only becomes beautiful and blesses others when it opens up and blooms. Its greatest tragedy is to stay in a tight-closed bud, never fulfilling its potential."
—*Anonymous*

In everything, give thanks to God! In every situation, let your words of praise resound and echo!

We now know why this is so important. We know the benefits and blessings that spring from this expression of our faith. We know the great good it carries for our lives. We know it's the right thing to do.

But even knowing this, I admit it isn't always easy. Giving thanks and praise can be a personal challenge—a real sacrifice—especially on those days and in those tough seasons when life's problems keep coming at you, constantly confronting and continually reaching out to try to steal your focus and joy. In those hard times, the last thing on our list is expressing our thanksgiving.

Despite the challenge, however, we can still do it. We can give thanks in the difficult hour. We can offer God our praise even when the circumstances appear dark and ominous. Thanks and praise, after all, is our way of faith—our way to see that bright white, beaming light that's there for us just ahead.

On the hard days and in the tough seasons, I like to hold the Bible in my hands. I can sense the weight of God's promises to me. By riffling the pages, I can hear the priceless sound of God's countless blessings for me.

This book in my hands is my book. It describes my citizenship, my royal standing, my eternal life. It tells the true story of my Savior, the Christ who came for me. It tells how Jesus came to rescue me, bless me, and empower me. He came to give me a new life—the new life in which I now stand.

The longer my hands hold this great book, the more thankful I become about my day and my circumstances. The longer I hold this book, the lighter and more insignificant my problems become. The more my hands grip the pages, the more grateful I am about all I've been given.

Today I'm united with God the Father and God the Son. Today I have their spirit, the Holy Spirit, living in me. Today I have the infinite resources of their kingdom. I've even been given the authority to speak on behalf of that kingdom—my kingdom. The authority to command, pronounce, and bless!

How can I not be thankful? How can I not give praise? I have so much.

With my empowerment, I can change, alter, and amend my earthly circumstances. I'm no longer powerless; I'm powerful because I have God's power to unleash good around me.

Just as importantly, my empowerment enables me to help others. I can assist, inspire, and benefit the lives of those I know and meet. What a day to be alive! What a day to express my thanks. Let me give thanks to God. Let me offer him my praise!

The Angry Minister Syndrome

Whenever I reflect on the new and empowered life you and I have been given as Christians, one story always comes to mind. It's the story of the Christian minister who was angry at God because of the condition of the world around him.

He was upset about the poverty and violence. He was upset about the injustice. He was upset about the large percentage of people living in ignorance without any knowledge of God or his promises.

The more this minister thought about the conditions and the circumstances on the earth, the more agitated he became. He wanted to know why God would allow such devastating problems to exist in so many places and so many lives.

Finally, as the minister's anger reached its peak, he barked out at God, saying, "God, what are you going to do about all this?"

God responded to the man: "My son, I've done everything I can do: I've given you my Son, his life, name, and authority. I've also given you my Word, my Spirit, and my faithfulness. It's in your hands. What are you going to do?"

What are we going to do? This question is inseparably linked to our empowerment, isn't it? It's up to us to trust and believe. It's up to us to speak and act. It's up to us to respond with the supernatural voice God has given each of us. We are heaven's agents on the earth, and it's in our hands to change the dire circumstances that surround us.

LIVING UP TO WHAT YOU'VE ALREADY ATTAINED

I appreciate how Paul encouraged us in our call to action. Focusing on our new life in Christ, Paul said, "Only let us live up to what we have already attained" (Phil. 3:16).

Paul's words are piercing, aren't they? Let us live up to what we've already attained, what we've already been given, what we already have. Let each of us grab hold and live the revolutionary life Christ has already secured for us. This new and empowered life is ours after all; it belongs to you and me.

And because it's ours, it's time—our time—to use and enjoy all we have. It's our time to fulfill our true potential in Christ. Our time to become who we already are in God's kingdom.

We know how. We know the way. In this book, we've studied and explored our walk of faith. We've learned about trusting God. We've learned about believing his promises. We understand the wisdom of taking in, storing up—of internalizing God's truths within us.

We also understand the other essential ingredient: the need to open our mouth—to put God's truths into action through our words, deeds, and daily attitude. We know God has designed our life of faith to be a powerful and dynamic life, one filled with vibrant, outward expression.

IT'S NEVER TOO LATE!

A wise and clever person once said, "It's never too late to be who you might have been."

That person was right . . . well, that person was right at least when it comes to what God has for those who are willing to trust him. For believers, it's never too late to become the person God has already planned and purposed us to be. As long as we have a breath in our lungs and a beat to our heart, it's never too late.

Ultimately, however, everything comes down to personal choices. We can choose to "live up to what we've already attained" or we can choose a different standard. We can choose to accept our potential in Christ or we can choose a different way. The choice is ours. The decision is ours.

Speaking for both my coauthor and myself, our sincerest hope is that you reach out today and grab hold of your full potential in Christ. Don't let the past get in your way. Don't let anything get in your way. We've all made mistakes, but that doesn't matter. What matters is what we choose for today.

Choose to take hold of your life in Christ. Choose to walk in all the gifts and provisions God has given you. Choose to be who you already are. Then go out and open your big, bold, beautiful mouth!

Personal Reflections

I choose to be who I already am in Christ!

I will open my big, bold, beautiful mouth to revolutionize my life and the world around me!